DRIVEN TO EXTREMES

DRIVEN TO EXTREMES

JEFF WALLACH

BURFORD BOOKS

Printed in the United States of America.

10   9   8   7   6   5   4   3   2   1

Library of Congress Cataloging-in-Publication Data
Wallach, Jeff.
    Driven to extremes : uncommon tales from golf's unmanicured terrain / Jeff Wallach.
        p.   cm.
    ISBN 1-58080-103-X
    1. Golf.   I. Title: Uncommon tales from golf's unmanicured terrain. II. Title.
GV965.W25   2002
796.352—dc21   2002002249

Versions of the following stories appeared (or are scheduled to appear) in these magazines:

Golf in the Institute; Fear and Loathing (mostly fear) in St. Andrews; and Metaphors Be with You, in *Inside Golf*.

Yippee Skippee; and Robert Trent Jones Jr. and the Edges of Doom, in *Acura Style*.

Heartland Golf School; Oregon Road Trip; and Whistler's (a) Mother, in *Maximum Golf*.

Old Works, New Tricks; Golfing Gourmet; Locals Rule: The Sure Bet of Las Vegas Golf; Wild A-Bandon; Just Deserts; Men in Green; Family Affair; Robert Trent Jones Jr. and the Edges of Doom; Playing Through; Golf Architecture's Biggest Fan; and Signature Hole, in *Links Magazine*.

From Slopes to Slope Ratings, in *Golf and Travel*.

Before the Fall; and Pioneering Canadian Golf, Ay?, in *National Golfer*.

The Wild and Ancient; in *Travel and Leisure Golf*.

When Irish Lies Are Smiling, in *Petersen's Golfing*.

Golf's Secret Garden, in *Sports Illustrated*.

With love for Reneé, my safe place

Other Books by Jeff Wallach

Beyond the Fairway: Zen Lessons, Insights,
and Inner Attitudes of Golf, Bantam Books, 1995

What the River Says: Whitewater Journeys Along
the Inner Frontier, Blue Heron Publishing, 1996

Breaking 100: Eugene Country Club's First Century,
Graphic Arts Center, 1999

TABLE OF CONTENTS

PART THREE: ECCENTRIC PERSONALITIES

Introduction:
Driven to Extremes

WHEN I FIND myself in certain circles—for example, among friends who kayak and rock climb and mountain bike, who travel to Burma and Burkina Faso and the Atlas Mountains—and I talk about golf, their eyes inadvertently roll back in their heads. Their expressions flatline. They'd as soon welcome a diatribe on the actuarial tables—or hammer a piton into their foreheads—as listen to anyone talk about golf.

By the same token, many of my golfing buddies get nervous when I suggest that they join me on some crazy backcountry odyssey that involves shooting rapids or camping on a mountaintop with no shower in sight. Their faces scrunch up as if I'm pulling their hair (or what's left of it). If they want adventure, these friends will watch Greg Norman try to win a major.

Needless to say, gathering these various cabals together at a party would be a recipe for disaster. What I can't get either group of friends to believe is that golf *is,* in many ways, an extreme sport—as you'll see in the pages that follow.

When I first began backpacking and running rivers in the desert Southwest fifteen years ago, I occasionally completed my wilderness journeys by visiting Moab Golf Club, a largely unknown track carved into red sandstone hills in southern Utah, and one of my favorites. If you wander into the scrubby flora off the thirteenth fairway, you might experience the kind of bizarre encounter that's described in chapter 17. Playing golf in Moab became, for me, a ritual of reentry to the world (or out of it, as some friends would contend) after spending time in remote canyonlands.

In those earlier years, the golf course parking lot was mostly filled with RVs and big-ass American cruisers, and the fairways were speckled with slow-moving herds of retirees. But more recently I've observed a startling increase in the ratio of dusty SUVs in the gravel lot. Many of these rigs sport bikes and kayaks strapped to the roof. If I peer through the windows, I spy climbing harnesses, ropes, telemark skis, battered Little Feat cassettes. Out on the golf course, I get matched up with river guides wearing Teva sandals.

Extreme-sports enthusiasts have finally begun to recognize the true nature of golf as an adventure activity in its own right. Granted, the actual physical dangers may prove less than, say, those presented by free-rappelling off a hundred-foot natural stone arch. But driving over a gaping arroyo and then draining your birdie putt to win a Nassau against your golfing nemesis can *feel* just as daunting. For proof, just check your pulse rate.

As a mediocre golfer, the game has always provided plenty of unexpected adventure for me—especially when I visit what I like to call the game's unmanicured terrain (I'm speaking metaphorically here, mostly). That's where you chance upon aspects of golf unlikely to appear at Pinehurst or Pebble Beach. As a journalist who's covered the sport in dozens of countries on four continents, my golf travels have led me to extremities of instruction, location, conditions, weather, companionship, and a large bucketful of ancillary variables. A healthy proportion of these exploits have occurred away from the clipped fairways of slickly run golf factories—in places like Moab, and Anaconda, Montana, and Africa—in the company of unlikely individuals, in environments and/or circumstances that nobody could ever have predicted or even made up.

The three sections of this book gather my own extreme-golf escapades into three categories: uncommon lessons; offbeat travels; and eccentric personalities. The stories in each section peek out from the tall fescues of the game's unmanicured terrain.

According to many editors I've worked with, whenever golf magazines survey their readers to find out what kinds of articles they prefer, the majority of folks say, "Bring on the instruction." In my own experience, most golf instruction could be used to anesthetize surgical patients. Which is to say most teaching pros emphasize the mechanical aspects of the golf swing, and most instructional books are sleepy manuals full of diagrams, technical terms, and photos of proper grip, stance, and alignment. While good mechanics are certainly important to playing well, traditional golf instruction ignores the facet of the sport that so many players most want to explore: the emotional and intellectual extremes where golf can serve as a vehicle to far more wide-ranging lessons.

Consider that on a typical Sunday the average golfer heads for his local course filled with optimism and confidence and fantasies of shooting an incredible round. Unfortunately, the odds are against him, because only about 10 percent of America's twenty-four million golfers actually even break a hundred on a regular basis—which suggests that the other 90 percent could benefit from some good instruction. But I'd rather shank a dump truck full of Pro-V1s into a scum-covered pond than endure a traditional golf lesson.

At the same time, even the most pitiful hacker occasionally executes a flawless shot that flies high and long, plunges onto the green with a pleasing thud, and bounds toward the pin. So virtually all players know they possess at least the potential to hit great shots. The fact that most golfers can't execute those shots consistently offers a clear golf lesson of its own: that playing well calls for mental proficiency, too. True students of the game recognize this as part of the Zen-like nature of golf. They know that excelling requires not only physical, but also metaphysical mastery.

In recent years more enlightened (or just plain wacky) golf instructors have begun teaching this aspect of the game in rather extreme ways. They may have students skipping and shouting like lunatics, *throwing* clubs at the driving range, hitting shots while blind-folded and standing on one leg, jumping off the top of perfectly good telephone poles, and otherwise acting in ways that will force anyone with any sense to inquire: What *on earth* could this possibly have to do with golf?

Part I of this book conveys strange tales of some of the most extreme golf lessons I've encountered. What they have in common is a dedication to using golf as a means, not an end. Instructors such as Fred Shoemaker, Ed LeBeau, and Chuck Hogan might as well be teaching French cooking classes or lanyard making or pumpkin carving; their particular focus on golf is essentially beside the point. What they offer is a path to mastery of something far beyond a particularly amusing and confounding ball-and-stick game.

The second section of this book is about extremes of golf travel, but by that I don't simply mean that the chapters describe what it was like playing in Mexico or Moab (although they do this, too). These stories range across North America and overseas to convey some highly unusual aspects of the game—from a course built atop a former EPA Superfund site to a new Las Vegas venue where virtually nobody is allowed to play; from an aerial golf adventure in Nova Scotia to a three-day competition played in sideways rain in Ireland. And as you'll see in the first chapter, even a visit to the most conservative bastion of the game—The Old Course at St. Andrews—has the power to startle. These stories highlight the extremes that are possible when you open yourself to the unexpected and venture, if I might borrow a phrase, beyond the fairway.

I don't need to tell you that golf attracts its share of fanatical per-sonalities—and I'm not just talking about head cases like John Daly or Seve Ballesteros. To view textbook examples of all manner of psy-choses, phobias, syndromes, obsessions, and compulsions, simply join any men's club and sign up for their Sunday game.

The third section of this book profiles a few of the more extreme characters I've encountered through golf—from poet and course architect Robert Trent Jones Jr. to my own friend Nate Dickinson, a retired millionaire who dreamed of a golf career . . . as a PGA Tour caddie. Of course, eccentric personalities also appear in the other sections, and some of them—friends such as John Hayden and fel-low golf writer Tom Harack—seem more than just coincidental bystanders in a number of my strange adventures.

Golf has begun to reinvent itself in recent years with the help of celebrities and superstar athletes who've taken up the game. But despite Charles Barkley, Dennis Hopper, Alice Cooper, and all the other unlikely suspects, you'll no doubt occasionally be faced with some eye-rolling skeptic (possibly one of my outdoor-oriented friends) who still thinks golf is staid, stupid, and deadly dull. If, by chance, this cynic uses the phrase *good walk spoiled,* you have my blessing to whap him with a flop wedge to ensure that he won't make that mistake again.

But the naysayers are right about this much: Golf *can* act as a powerful sedative (especially *watching* golf, for godsakes!) if you fail to treat it as the adventure it's got the potential to be. So I encour-age you to drive yourself into unmanicured terrain and experience a few of the game's many extremes for yourself.

As one rocker-statesman once put it, "That's where the fun is."

PART ONE

Uncommon Lessons

1

Golf in the Institute:
Shivas Irons Goes to Esalen

In the same way that looking for the perfect golf swing outside ourselves is inconsistent and frustrating, so, too is seeking an identity from the outside world, and these two things are connected in a meaningful way. Our identity is vitally important to us—it's our uniqueness, our individuality—and the quest for self identity extends to games, as well.

Your thoughts, attitudes, and emotions may change when you hit a bad golf shot, but there is a part of you that doesn't change. That is the deepest part of you, and when you can experience it, and play golf from it, you will have tapped into the source of consistency. Your golf will no longer be a search for who you are; it will be an expression of who you are.

—FRED SHOEMAKER, Extraordinary Golf

THE ROAD SOUTH from the Monterey Peninsula in California—away from Pebble Beach and Spanish Bay, and toward the hippie surfer enclave of Big Sur—begs for loud music filled with percussion. As I swung my old Subaru into the curves, cornering hard and gazing beyond the crumbling shoulder to where cliffs dropped precipitously down to the blue Pacific, I pounded on the steering wheel

and sang along with Steve Winwood about being back in the high
life again.

I was headed for the Esalen Institute—pure stereotypical California: organic food; bizarre workshops; sandals; old guys with beards
and Ph.D.'s, and young women in blowsy skirts and no bras and
Ph.D.'s, all edging toward enlightenment. A cross between a new-age
commune and an academic think tank, reputed magnet for free
thinkers, free lovers, and freeloaders, where people introduce themselves as "Sunflower" or "Two Birds." A destination of extraordinary
beauty and power perched on cliffs above surf crashing against the
very edge of the continent, nestled between high rounded mountains and redwood forests, where a clear stream roars down a steep
canyon and guests soak at night in warm mineral baths beneath a sky
full of shooting stars.

I felt cheerful and optimistic as I cruised the coastal highway seeking the entrance to Esalen. The sun glowed warm on my elbow poking
out the window, and cool spray rose up in the salt air and life was good.

Still, at the same time that I enjoyed a salad of leafy green emotions, my intellect was simultaneously overengaged—analyzing and
interpreting my feelings, shopping for details I might later use to
describe my experiences. As Steve Winwood broke into "Higher
Love" I leaned over and scribbled in my notebook: "THE ROAD SOUTH
FROM MONTEREY BEGS FOR LOUD MUSIC FILLED WITH PERCUSSION."

While most of the other folks I encountered at Esalen over the
next week were visiting from across the United States, from various
other continents, and even from several unidentified planets of their
own personal habitation to study ecstatic dance or shamanic rituals,
or to integrate their chakras, I'd embarked upon this pilgrimage for
a different but equally spiritual reason. As I registered with the long-
haired security guard at the front gate, I thought I detected a dis-
dainful smile when I announced that I'd come for the golf.

Although Esalen has no golf course or practice range or even
much grass of the kind you could hit balls off, twice annually it hosts

a five-day seminar called the Golf in the Kingdom (GITK) Workshop, named after the mystical book written by Michael Murphy more than two decades ago. The book relates the story of the narrator's brief life-altering visit to Scotland during which a local golf pro revealed the spirit of the game and showed him how golf can provide a vehicle for journeying both inwardly and into cosmic realms. It is the kind of book that people whisper the title of. Fans have even formed the Shivas Irons Society, to celebrate the evanescent whiskey-drinking golf pro who teaches the young traveler the meaning of golf. Author Murphy also happened to have cofounded Esalen—a perfect synchronicity. *Golf in the Kingdom* and the Esalen workshop of the same name are about golf in the same way that *Moby-Dick* is a book about fishing.

But Murphy's—and Esalen's—connection to the game was lost on many of the other guests I met at the institute, who seemed more than skeptical that golf could constitute a spiritual path. In fact, most other Esalenites treated us golfers as pariahs in collared shirts sporting the names of expensive resorts.

At dinner my first night, the woman sitting across from me dug into her vegetable stew and asked what workshop I was attending. When I explained she lamented, "So I guess you're not into feelings."

Throughout our stay I overheard various guests—folks who would be ridiculed mercilessly at a country club and might defend themselves by advocating openness and nonjudgment—refer scornfully to "the golfers." When a man wearing a dozen earrings and a tie-dyed skirt expressed surprise to see chicken on the mostly vegetarian menu one night, his companion—dressed in a loincloth, for godsakes—shrugged and said by way of explanation: "The golfers." It probably didn't help our cause that during two different exercises in our workshop, a golf ball and a golf club accidentally flew over a group of naked sunbathers and splashed into the swimming pool.

If GITK wasn't your traditional golf school, our instructors weren't exactly a group of lanky cardboard PGA stiffs, either. They were a foursome of diverse, creative, and inspiring individuals who traveled without kitschy swing aids and had no products to sell.

Andy Nusbaum, formerly with Golf Digest Schools, looked like the quintessential golf instructor: tall, thin, soft-spoken, and reserved, with a hint of a southern accent. But Andy helped us get a grip rather than working on our grips. He'd recently quit his job in Connecticut and was relocating to California to "follow his bliss."

Brian Bergstrom, formerly a jazz musician and now a massage therapist, provided stretching and other exercises to ensure that our physical bodies accompanied our metaphysical ones along the path. Brian was a large, strong, gentle fellow with a pixie grin, a capable but inconsistent golfer who could bend a two-iron shot around trees and onto the green from 240 yards away but who might whiz his next shot deep into the shrubbery—and still manage to remain good-natured. Brian provided a bridge between GITK's sometimes esoteric teaching and the plane that most of the rest of us inhabit on the golf course.

Steve Cohen, a Gestalt therapist, was unlikely to be giving lessons in any sport: portly, tight, intense beneath a calm exterior, and an average golfer, he challenged us to explore difficult personal issues. He pushed us in a way that was extremely supportive and respectful of our boundaries. The founder of the Shivas Irons Society, Steve first came to Esalen as a dishwasher back in the 1970s.

But Fred Shoemaker, brilliant teacher, author of the book *Extraordinary Golf,* a modest wizard in khaki pants, was the turbocharger on the engine of the workshop. Fred offered new ways of looking at things that we encountered every day without really seeing. He is the kind of teacher who manages to impart wisdom that you don't even realize you've learned—a sort of time-released instruction that even months later continued to cure some of the ills in my golf game and in my life. Fred was kind, funny, insightful, and irreverent; he struck me as always likely to be the inexplicable factor in wonderful things. He managed to show us—through action stories (he is the King of Zen-like parables)—rather than telling us the things we needed to learn.

Our group of students consisted of fourteen men (though women often attend GITK) ranging in age from twenty-something to eighty, educated and professional but spanning a wide political and spiritual spectrum, encompassing both sarcastic conservatives who smoked cigarettes and gulped Scotch on the patio late at night and meditative lotus-perching Esalen devotees. Individuals possessing various ideas and histories and intentions, exhibiting a seemingly limitless range of flaws in our golf swings and our personal lives, yet all sharing one vision: We cared about golf and believed it held possibilities that we hoped that our instructors could help us unlock.

I felt a part of the group but also removed, because although I'd traveled to Esalen to face some of my own challenges in and through golf, I was also there as an observer—the journalist—an artificial dichotomy that would prove challenging in the workshop and throughout my personal life.

The evening of our arrival we gathered in the carpeted Huxley Room, which was lined with mirrors and giant throw pillows. In his introductory remarks, Fred Shoemaker talked about how on the golf course most of us are: (1) uncommitted, except to looking good; (2) constantly judging ourselves; and (3) always on the verge of being upset—which pretty much summed up my game. He also observed that after executing a bad shot most golfers are afraid they'll do the same thing again. Fred suggested that we needed to see our futures as not determined by our past so as to keep possibilities open.

"Wouldn't it be great," he asked us, "if we could walk up to the first tee and instead of saying that we probably won't play well because we just bought new clubs, or our back hurts, we could say that our whole lives we've been afraid of what other people might be thinking of us, and we're really fucking tired of it?"

Not the sort of commentary you'd expect from your typical golf pro. But neither were many of the drills we performed over the next five days: howling, punching pillows, role playing, spending almost an entire morning at a nearby practice facility without hitting any balls, being videotaped throwing our clubs.

That first night Steve Cohen explained that the intent of the workshop was to bring awareness to areas of behavior, and to the golf swing, to create the possibility of change. Without awareness, change can't take place. Awareness, Steve told us, is essential to all spiritual practice and growth.

Toward that end, he led us through a series of interpersonal exercises designed to focus our awareness on things that were real and directly in front of us in the room. One was designed to show us how we make up stories about things and each other, rather than simply being aware.

To illustrate this point Fred told us to imagine that we were pulling into a crowded parking lot in our car, and just as we were going to park in the last empty space, a guy in a red convertible zipped in front of us and grabbed it. Then he jumped out of his car and ran into a nearby building.

Awareness mode would teach us to simply note what had happened, but our instinct to make up stories might lead us to think: *Asshole!* But what if we learned that he was actually rushing insulin to his mother because she'd lapsed into a diabetic coma, or some such thing? The stories we constantly make up are often just as wrong. So, too, Fred told us, is the story that because we slice a tee shot—or five tee shots—we're lousy golfers. Our judgments and stories separate us from a reality that is truly free of these fictions. Our task is to let go of such stories and simply be aware of what *is*.

He posited that our cultural view is like a pair of glasses we can't take off, and that in golf this view manifests as a notion that there's something wrong with our game that we must fix. The first step in changing is becoming aware of this culture, and then becoming aware of a new culture—in this case that there is simply something going on in our swing that we must be aware of. Awareness leads to consistency and improvement, and it allows the body's natural instincts to come into play. These make the swing more powerful and efficient.

Fred also talked about how we all possess blind spots in our putting strokes, in our full swings, and in our lives—places where we aren't aware of what's happening. Yet since we can only try to "fix" what we're aware of, we tinker with the parts of the swing we already know, though potential problems may lie elsewhere. Fixing things is the wrong approach, and never works. The task of any good instructor, according to the GITK gospel, is to help bring awareness to our blind spots, thereby making miraculous transformation possible. Trying to fix something specific because we already know that thing is like taking our car to a mechanic who only knows how to fix carburetors. Which is fine, unless we happen to have any other of a thousand possible problems.

By simply being aware of something like a bad shot, without making up the story that we are lousy golfers—which in itself usually leads us to try to fix what we think is wrong—we really make change possible. In relating this to the golf swing Fred said, "How can you fix something when you don't know what it is? How can you correct what you're doing when you don't have any idea what you're doing? You cannot fix your golf swing unless you know what your golf swing is. Awareness is the only thing that allows for development."

We ended our first session by standing in a circle and clasping hands. Steve asked us to imagine energy flowing like white light from our hearts, out our left hands, and into the next man, and in through our right hands from the man on that side.

We also shared our goals for the next few days and the gifts we'd come here to give ourselves. I was surprised that several men had come to the workshop because they were at critical junctures in their lives. One man's marriage was in trouble. A young guy named Bob had recently quit his Wall Street job and didn't know what to do next. He'd given himself this week to simply stop worrying and try to be who he was. When my turn came, I said that I hoped to be able to use golf to get out of my head and into my heart, and to lose self-consciousness, which was a lifelong struggle in golf and in my life.

The mood was a little fluffy, but also ripe with the sense that anything could happen and probably would. While most of us, I think it's safe to say, were excited by the prospect of learning golf in such a way that we might receive important insights that applied to the rest of our lives, not everyone was absolutely goosey at the start. If Bob (who later earned the nickname Bogey Bob), for example, represented the spontaneous and receptive extreme on the openness spectrum, Simon—a former wildlife biologist who'd come to GITK to learn techniques he might put to use in his new career as a golf instructor—harbored some serious questions about what he'd gotten himself into. He figured that if we were all standing around holding hands after just a couple of hours, we might very well be screwing each other by day five. He considered driving fast back out the gate that very night, but his unrequitable love of golf convinced him to stick around for at least another day.

We finished our session at around ten. The property was quiet, though you could hear hushed voices from where groups and couples gathered on the lawns, or walked in the garden. I felt fresh and alive as I went back to my room, retrieved a towel, and headed down to the baths for a hot soak.

Walking across the dark property beneath a sliver of moon, it occurred to me that perhaps I'd chosen a writing career because it provided the perfect way for me to hide within my mind and not get in touch with and reside in my feelings. Instead of opting for awareness, I'd chosen a career that was essentially based on making up stories.

I also thought about how earlier in the evening, when we'd stood in the circle, Steve had asked us on the count of three to howl or snort or cry or scream, and I'd waited to see how spontaneously the others sounded off before letting go even a little bit myself. This type of control seemed closely related to my role as the journalist, too. I thought to write this in my notebook, but I'd left it back in my room.

The next morning the grass glistened with dew as I hurried across the lawn to grab a cup of coffee before reporting for a 7 A.M. stretching class. After that we ate breakfast and then spent most of the morning putting back in Huxley with the doors open to the sound of the ocean. We didn't putt to hone our accuracy, but to simply feel freedom and experience letting go. We swung the putter until it just felt good.

Fred also gave us a couple of putting exercises designed to increase our awareness. We concentrated on seeing light glistening on the ball's dimples, and how half the ball lay in shadow like the dark side of a full moon. We practiced walking to the hole with our eyes closed to learn to feel distance. We putted while keeping our eyes on where the ball had been before we hit it, and then tried to sense where it ended up in relation to the hole. Our instructors encouraged us to see the hole as the center of a broader area, not the end, and they suggested that most golfers leave their putts short because they are afraid of the unknown.

Fred's advice on putting was simple and concise: "Putting is not a function of time and practicing, but about eliminating interference. And the way to putt is the way to do everything else." He also reminded us that a missed putt was simply a missed putt.

In the afternoon Fred developed his theory about awareness, blind spots, and interference in greater detail by showing us some video he'd shot that morning, after we'd finished putting and gone outside to the practice net set up on the lawn. Simon must have finally thought he was going to receive the kind of hands-on golf instruction he craved.

For each student, Fred first rolled tape of us hitting golf balls and asked whether we were aware of some particular aspect of our swing—a goofy loop, an over-the-top move, the way an arm bent or didn't bend. He didn't imply that anything was "wrong" with the particular swing component; he simply sought to focus our awareness on something we hadn't noticed before.

After running slow-motion segments of us hitting golf balls, Fred then revealed some of the most shocking video that any of us had ever seen: frames in which—at Fred's request—we'd taken normal backswings and then flung our clubs at a target. Without exception, every last one of us—even the guys who owned swings that were as painful to watch as an ugly child—suddenly displayed the most naturally graceful and elegant motions imaginable. When Fred juxtaposed our hitting swings beside our club-throwing swings, the difference was so severe as to seem almost comical. We oohed. We ahhed. We guffawed. We shook our heads in wonder and disbelief.

A particular highlight was when Paul, a journalist for the *L.A. Times,* experienced a bit of trouble letting go (apparently a common ailment among journalists). His late release during the club toss caused his five-iron to flap out of control like a wounded waterfowl and land with a splash in the swimming pool. Although the club's flight wasn't caught on film, we enjoyed watching the close-up of Paul's reaction.

The club toss was so simple yet serendipitous. Fred posited that besides demonstrating the importance of letting go (literally, but also of performance, ego attachment, mechanics, and other "interference") the club toss provided irrefutable evidence that we each already possess a natural, near-perfect swing that is exactly right for us. He called it our "Original Swing" and suggested that our bodies know how to execute this swing once we remove all the interference that arises when we're addressing a golf ball. Interference—in both golf and life—consists of things we've been told by other people, parental or societal voices that try to insist we do things a certain way even when we know somewhere inside us how to do these things better or more naturally. An essential objective of the entire GITK Workshop was to remove interference and restore our Original Swings rather than inundating us with mechanics that weren't our own. Which would serve to reunite us with deeply buried parts of ourselves.

Fred was intense and emotional talking about the Original Swing. "It's not out there," he told us. "There's nothing outside yourself that you have to find. But there's nothing in our culture that gives that message.

"So believe nothing. Trust no one—only your own experience. Learning never takes place through information. And this is about learning. Repetition doesn't matter; waking up does. We only know the Western view of effort. But this is the real effort. Everything else is just stories." Fred explained that we have to play golf out of the same part of us that grows hair and breathes—not the "I" we're familiar with, but the one that can act spontaneously and live without interference.

After we finished watching the videos, our instructors invented a makeshift four-hole golf course across the lawn, over the swimming pool, and around the various naked bodies taking in the sun. The flag sticks looked lovely against a backdrop of people silently practicing tai chi.

The tiny course was among the most beautiful I'd ever been lucky enough to swing a club on. Waves crashed whitely on the rocks far below the edge of one fairway. Behind the second green, melons and wildflowers, herbs and cabbages, garlic and stone goddesses commingled in perfect harmony in the giant garden, and the air was perfumed with oregano, cilantro, and mint. Birds hummed and bickered in the pines and a cool breeze offset the warm California sun.

Despite this dreamy environment, I still managed to worry about duffing a chip shot or shanking a seven-iron out of bounds; I was still focused on performance, but at least now I'd brought awareness to this aspect of my character, and I knew what I most needed to let go of—a challenge that would continue to dog me for a long time.

In the evening we met back in our seminar room for Steve Cohen's Gestalt visualization session—another exercise you're unlikely to encounter at your local golf school. Steve told Paul and me that we couldn't bring our notebooks—which I found very liberating. As soon as I put mine aside I became emotionally centered and connected, and began to really feel the things that transpired among us in that closed room.

As we lay on our backs on the carpeted floor, eyes closed, breathing deeply into our stomachs, Steve encouraged us to imagine ourselves golfing on a beautiful course. What did it look like? Who showed up to play along with us? Who cheered—or heckled us—from the gallery? Steve's voice was hypnotic, and transported me away . . .

I found myself on a gorgeous rugged desert layout reminiscent of the Boulders Resort course outside Scottsdale, Arizona. As I stood on the first tee, my father emerged from the clubhouse and strolled toward me with his clubs. I smiled as I welcomed him, but also experienced resignation over the nature of our relationship and the understanding that at this point in our lives it was unlikely to change. But I accepted this, and felt joy that he'd come to play golf with me. Then two close friends—John and David—appeared on the tee and we all played the first hole.

John and I made birdies on the long par four. My dad rattled the flag on his third shot and then knocked in the putt for par. David, who doesn't even really play golf, managed a respectable bogey. Every girlfriend I've ever had looked on from behind the gallery ropes.

As we walked off the green, my friends and I headed for the next tee, but for some reason my father had to leave. At first I was afraid because I interpreted this as a premonition of his death. But then I came to see our parting as a different sort of good-bye; my father, who is not inclined toward self-examination, simply could not travel on the path that the rest of us—through therapy and adventure travel and various other forms of exploration (including golf)—had chosen to pursue. I was sad that my father couldn't share the journey, but I was grateful to have played this golf hole with him. I experienced a peaceful acceptance, followed by excitement about continuing our game.

When Steve Cohen's soft voice summoned us back from our visualizations, we gathered in a circle and talked about where we'd been. Fathers were common visitors in our experiences. One man recalled how he'd always loved playing golf with his dad, and how just before he died, they'd gone out to play together; the son hit nearly all the shots because his father was too weak to swing, but once they reached the green, his father stroked the putts.

With Steve's guidance, another man confronted his father's spirit in our presence, beginning rationally but ultimately cursing him for being such a critical and oppressive influence in his life, saying, "I hate your fucking guts." Steve encouraged him to pursue this, but he'd gone as far as he wanted to.

Bogey Bob had a particularly moving experience, collapsing into tears in a breakdown that was also obviously a breakthrough. In fact, many of us cried, either during our own stories or while listening to the pain of others. My heart went out to these men and I saw how ludicrous and inaccurate my stories about them had been: that one was cold and superior; that another just wasn't smart enough to really be engaged. That another didn't like me.

I also found it amazing that our lives and deep feelings were so inextricably connected to this crazy game. When I asked Steve about this exercise later, he explained that reaching out through a visualization and embracing a parent or friend or even a part of yourself that you've been judgmental of, or lacked closure with, can lead to self-acceptance. Which makes it easier for us to live freely and without interference. These little visualized mini vacations can provide another way of discovering our Original Swings. Of course the exercise didn't need to have anything to do with golf—that was just our vehicle.

But in terms of the game, such events would show results, Steve said. "From there, lower scores just happen. If you write, the words flow. If you go out in business, you get more contracts."

Still, Simon and maybe a few of the others had come to Esalen to learn something practical about a particular game played with a little white ball. As he told me later about the workshop, "All the golf stuff was great, but I didn't like the parts where it seemed as if we were on a psychiatrist's couch. We created an atmosphere where personal issues were much easier to talk about. But I thought deeply that I didn't have these sorts of unresolved issues, that I had nothing to open up about. I still can't bring myself to say that it had anything to do with what I wanted. That deep, intimate stuff was very uncomfortable. I felt sorry for the individuals, and I didn't think it belonged. I wanted more hands-on instruction. It was interesting, but what did it have to do with golf?"

The following morning we gathered outside the dining room after breakfast as four volunteer drivers from our group pulled up in their cars. We loaded in our golf bags and headed out to the Rancho Cañada golf course, an hour away in Carmel.

We spent the entire morning on the range, mostly without even hitting golf balls. Fred assigned us each a partner with whom we worked on awareness of the personal swing component that he'd pointed out in our videos. Mine was a weird pop-up that occurred in the transition zone when the clubhead reached its apex at the top of my backswing. On the tape, I'd seen how this could cause me to come over the top and slice. My partner Mike, an earnest and patient accountant, exhibited a weird elbow drop. We took turns observing each other and either supporting or contradicting the swinger's observation as to whether or not the swing glitch occurred.

For much of the morning I simply couldn't feel the club popping up in the transition zone. Even Mike had a hard time detecting it at first. Fred came by to remind us that we were trying to develop awareness, not to fix anything.

Of course I recognized that Fred knew what was "wrong" with each of our swings, but by simply putting our awareness in that area, he made it possible for us to learn experientially, so that the learning was wholly our own. As Steve Cohen said, "Fred can look at the swing and know ten things to improve, but that doesn't do any good at all. If you can be aware of even one area, that makes all the difference in the world."

Mike demonstrated incredible patience as I struggled to develop awareness of this blind spot in my swing. Eventually, Brian Bergstrom recognized my difficulties and offered a sort of translation of what Fred was trying to get me to see. Brian suggested that I think of my backswing as a clock in such a way that bringing the club back parallel to the ground equaled twelve noon. He asked what time I thought I was swinging to.

"About noon," I said, and he and Mike looked at each other with surprise.

"That's about three-thirty in the afternoon," Mike said, and Brian nodded. Then he suggested that maybe I should focus my awareness on where the club ended up in my backswing, and Mike could confirm or contradict what I observed, which would facilitate my awareness. Brian didn't imply that swinging past noon was bad; he just suggested I'd benefit from being more aware of where the club was at any given time.

Part of me analyzed the input I'd received and concluded that Fred and Brian were really implying that I was taking the club back too far. I understood that I'd been coiling my muscles too tight with such a large backswing, and the muscles couldn't hold the tension, and so the club recoiled, or popped up, to release some of the strain. But I chose to ignore this and simply work on trying to be aware of what time I was swinging to. When I managed to be able to recognize a swing to twelve noon, and then turned back to the pop-up, it wasn't happening anymore. But at some level I still struggled to understand this intellectually.

After lunch, we actually went out on the golf course to play a game recommended by Shivas Irons in *Golf in the Kingdom*. We were to play three holes for centering, three for true gravity, and three for score. The parameters seemed forced to me, especially as I wanted to let go of all this and just play golf. But I also wanted to score well and impress my fellow students. My notions of letting go of performance and score were false, I realized, because I wanted to accomplish these things so that I might score better. My culture of performance was very hard to give up. The paradox was that I'd have to *genuinely* not care about score to ever score better.

And the paradox was the same for my writing: Until I stopped thinking at every moment about how I'd write about something later, I'd never live in the moment fully enough to have pure experiences to write about. This was what Hemingway meant when he said that once you talked about a thing you ruined it.

That night we ate dinner at Fred's house outside Carmel. I asked him about the club-throwing thing and why it worked so well—was it a coincidence, a gift from the golf gods, was there a kind of quantum physics behind it, or what? Fred laughed and then told me to just get out of my fucking head. "You can't figure out how to do it, but you can do it," he said. "Understanding is the lowest step on the way to learning."

The next day was mostly free for us to roam the institute grounds, get massages, and otherwise infiltrate and scare the Esalen populace. Fred offered some optional informal lessons in Huxley. When I dropped in on them for a little while after meditating in a quiet hut beside the roaring stream, and walking for an hour in the redwood grove upcanyon, he was teaching some of the others how to hit with more power by changing their swings in such a way that the *whoosh* occurred during and after impact, rather than in the early downswing.

In the late afternoon I climbed down the cliff stairs, past a reflecting pool full of blooming lotus flowers, and sat on the beach watching with childlike amazement as the waves hit the rocks in bursts of spray like a clubhead hitting a ball. It occurred to me then that in a purely Zen golf workshop we might never even talk about golf swings or scores; we'd discuss the ocean waves, or the grass growing. Which is a way that Fred taught: expressing plenty of deeply Zen concepts without ever talking about Zen. As a student, I felt I should respond in kind without dragging the teachings down by analyzing them and describing them as Zen-like.

After breakfast on our last full day we drove back out to Rancho Canada for the Esalen Scramble—our ritual of passage.

Earlier in the week, Simon had asked what such activities as our Gestalt session had to do with golf. He might as well have asked what the Esalen Scramble had to do with joy, magic, letting go, living up to our potential, and feeling deeply connected to others through this outwardly simple game.

The Scramble format was based on four-man best ball, but included an added twist: Your team could subtract an extra stroke on any hole that each shot you used had been hit by a different player. I didn't care for this at first because it took away the chance for individual glory—which, of course, was the entire ego-stealing, performance-squelching point. We also had to use three drives from each player; had to hit a hook off the tee on one hole, and a slice on another; and had to play a particular long par four with a single club.

I must report that despite my skepticism, for the first time since beginning to play golf at the age of twelve I experienced a tsunami of delight on the golf course so overwhelming as to seem hallucinatory. Four of us who, averaged together, could only be described as slightly better than mediocre, somehow managed to shoot sixteen under par, or fifty-six. Upon finishing this unforgettable round I looked at the scorecard with detachment, as if it hadn't been me out there draining six high-pressure putts and coming through on the seventeenth hole by cracking a 230-yard uphill approach shot out of the rough to an elevated, well-protected green, and landing it five feet from the pin after my partners had all missed their attempts. But I came to see that of course it was me—the very best part of me, the part that rarely appears because of interfering self-consciousness and concerns about performance. But today, playing mostly from aware-ness mode, I'd excelled.

That night, as we sat in a circle back in the Huxley Room at Esalen waiting for our instructors to announce the winner of the competition and bestow the first prize, I knew that no other group could have performed the way we had. But I also recognized that it didn't really matter; I'd just enjoyed the most blessed round of golf in my life. So when Fred—after building up the suspense over which foursome had set a new Esalen Scramble record—simply tossed all the scorecards in the air to facilitate our letting go, I watched them flutter above us and felt a loosening of my grip of attachment, a fis-sure in my armor, a true release that was like a reunion with a child-like part of myself that I'd chased angrily out of my own yard many years ago.

Not even Simon sneaked over to where the scorecards lay scat-tered on the floor to see who had won.

On our final morning I woke early and ate breakfast alone and took my coffee down to a rock perched near the edge of the cliff overlooking the ocean. Not far from me a wild free-form dance class was snaking its way around the swimming pool. I saw Bogey Bob there, contorting in ecstasy, his eyes closed, oblivious to what he might have looked like, inhabiting a world of pure feeling.

Soon after, when our group met back in Huxley for the last time, Steve led a short visualization in which we imagined ourselves in a safe place. I saw myself in the yard of my childhood home. I must have been about two or three years old—just able to stand without falling over. My mother and I were batting a giant beach ball back and forth, and I was mesmerized by the revolving colors and the feeling of knocking the ball back and forth with this person who loved me unconditionally. There was no worry about hitting or not hitting, no consciousness, even, except the pure joy of the activity. It was unlike any other experience in sport I'd ever had, and I recognized the value of being able to feel that my performance didn't matter at all.

Then we sat and talked about the past week, and the gifts we'd received.

Bob broke into tears again describing the freedom he'd experienced. He said the workshop let him be who he really was, and that wasn't a Wall Street broker. Esalen made golf a game for him again and reminded him of how much he really loved sports. He also said that playing with Fred had been like playing with a Zen master.

"You golf the way you go through life," Bob explained. "The way you interrelate with others, or react to good or bad events. It enlightened me to know this. Once I paid attention to it, it was really powerful. I decided to let down and be whoever I wanted to be, and go with whatever happened. I never felt that before. I never before opened up without holding back."

When Simon's turn came around, he talked about how his ideas had been getting smashed in the workshop all week, but now he saw ways to glue the shell back together. He was a bird expert, so this was a perfect analogy. But Steve took this a step further by suggesting that Simon forget "fixing" the egg and instead pay attention to what might be hatching from it.

I had occasion to speak to Simon a couple of months after GITK, and while he was grateful to have garnered a few new techniques for increasing his distance off the tee and for use with his own golf students, he'd also discovered something unexpected. Remembering the experience with great fondness, he admitted, "As I've changed my golf attitude, I have changed as well. It's made me a more open person, though I still have a channel where enough is enough. But maybe where Steve was going that night of the Gestalt session—just maybe—that's one channel I haven't unlocked."

When it was my turn to speak, I started by thanking my instructors for the things they'd taught me, but I also realized that a deep understanding might have led me to simply demonstrate in some powerful way, rather than talking analytically, about what I'd learned. I considered smacking Fred with a putter in the manner of enlightened Zen students in ancient Japanese koans. But that moment of insight gave way to analysis and judgment and stories, and I determined that such an action would seem crazy, and maybe my instructors wouldn't even understand it.

So I told the group that what I needed to do at that very moment was to stand up and leave the circle, walk out the door and across the wide lawn to the fence at the very edge of the cliff, and just rear back and fucking *fling* my notebook out into the void.

I felt a huge surge of energy in my chest as I said this, and at the same time I winged my notebook above the circle. It flew erratically, the pages flapping, and landed with a thud against the mirror on the far wall. Later, several of the others told me that this was an intensely liberating moment for them, full of power and exactly the kind of thing that best expressed the character of the workshop.

But I knew that I'd not only been worried about being overdramatic and about what the others might think; I also knew that I'd been even more concerned about how I'd ever remember all the important things I'd written if I really threw my notebook off the cliff. I'd backed away from the action that would have liberated me, and instead I gave into analysis and other interference.

Instead of walking to the brink and taking decisive and pure action, I talked about it, and then scribbled in my notebook, "TOSSED NOTEBOOK!"

2

Yippee Skippee:
Chuck Hogan Has Golf on the Brain

I sense that every aspect of the gull's life, of the storm's life, of the planet's itself, was play. Hunting and killing included. It was all play. . . . This play was, I could see, not in any sense inferior to "work." It was superior. An aspect of devotion, holy in itself, but more than that, absolutely necessary in the cosmic scheme. As if the gears of the universe itself depended on these gulls wheeling in the wind and us humans enmeshed as intimately in that same wind and field.
—STEVEN PRESSFIELD, *The Legend of Bagger Vance*

Play on the surface. The work takes place beneath. Growth of intelligence is never a conscious process; conceptual changes always take place below awareness. —JOSEPH CHILTON PEARCE, *Magical Child*

AS I WALKED alongside one of the smooth, rolling, perfectly groomed fairways at the Raven Golf Club in south Phoenix, I tried not to be alarmed by the strange sounds emanating from the practice stations at the adjacent learning center. Although it occurred to me that perhaps someone had sprung the lunatics from the asylum for golf lessons today, I learned that it was only Chuck Hogan, shouting high-pitched "yippees!" into the warm, dry air, slapping his students with double high-fives, and dancing around on the grass.

Hogan, whose bulldog posture and gentle smile suggest a warm-hearted football coach, and whose eyebrows are a marvel of jungle-thick proportion, was at that time running the Raven's Golf Learning Center. Founder of the Chuck Hogan Golf Schools, an organization called Sports Enhancements Associates, and a nonprofit institute called Athletics and the Intelligence of Play, and guru to such touring pros as Peter Jacobsen, D. A. Wiebring, and Grant Waite, Hogan makes even most alternative golf instructors seem conservative and quaint. It's not just his manner but his ideas that place Chuck on the farthest fringe of the outer edges of the world of golf and explain the fond, cryptic smiles that appear on golfers' faces whenever his name comes up. As one of the pioneers of alternative golf instruction Chuck is like that lone figure behind the wheel of a tractor out on the driving range, methodically performing his job while everyone takes aim at him. But he's proved an elusive target.

Hogan espouses two main concepts in his teaching: that we must learn to use our brains better to become better learners (of golf and everything else); and that many of us experience mental problems on the golf course and elsewhere because, as children, we never felt safe enough to just play. Chuck is big on play, and there is something almost alarmingly childlike about him, even separate from his "yippees!" on the practice range.

Much of Hogan's teaching philosophy is based on a book called *Magical Child,* by Joseph Chilton Pearce. In Chuck's typical superlative-espousing fashion, he calls it "the most important piece of literature—scriptural or nonscriptural—in existence on our planet, by a hundred or a thousand times." Pearce's book describes the biological processes by which our brains develop, and how these processes relate to the social bonding that we experience early in life.

After I talked about this and other subjects with Chuck several times on the phone long distance, he finally agreed to spend some time with me in Phoenix if I would submit to two conditions: (1) that he could terminate our interview at any moment, without warning or reason; and (2) that if, in working with me, he suggested some dramatic change in my diet or other routines, for example, I promised to adopt his recommendations. Otherwise, we'd have nothing further to discuss.

Despite the eccentricity his demands implied, Chuck seemed relatively normal, reasonable, and soft-spoken when I first met him in person for breakfast in the Raven's sunny grill room one morning. I resisted ordering eggs and sausage out of fear that he might command me to stop eating fat, cholesterol, and meat. Chuck ordered French toast and doused it with syrup and butter. As we warmed to our conversation and the waitress filled our coffee cups, I tried to steer him into a discussion about sports psychology, but he had his own subject matter in mind. He wanted to talk about the brain.

To give me an idea of his teaching philosophy, Chuck summarized some of the brain-related concepts in Pearce's book. Over his French toast (which I coveted from behind my fruit plate) he explained that birth—our journey from the safe, quiet environment of the womb into a noisy and unpredictable world full of stimuli— is possibly the most stressful experience that humans ever encounter. But at the same time, stress produces a chemical called ACTH, which is essential to the growth of our brains. ACTH milenates or coats neural connections in the brain, which in essence strengthens the intricate network along which electrical impulses travel when we think or act. Which is to say that stress is not only necessary but crucial for our brains to develop.

Chuck further explained that stress occurs when we perceive a threat with one of our senses: We hear a crashing sound close by, or see someone running toward us with a gun, or smell smoke. The stress elicited by such stimuli causes production of ACTH, which in turn increases and strengthens the connections between neurons. But whereas stress is essential to our development, in our society we experience a great deal of anxiety, the difference being that although anxiety creates a similar sense of threat, its source is purely imagined. There's no sensory evidence to back it up. Like when we're standing over a two-foot putt to win a five-dollar Nassau and suddenly feel afraid. According to Chuck, anxiety not only doesn't produce ACTH to milenate neuronal connections, but may also actually cause the production of unhealthy chemical toxins.

After birth, Chuck continued, the most natural and healthy stress occurs when a young human begins to explore outward from a safe place into the unknown, moving back and forth between the two as he becomes more comfortable. For the youngest children, biology predisposes their mothers to provide that safe place in the form of a bond of complete and unconditional acceptance and love. With this relationship providing emotional and physical security, the child can confidently crawl around in the stress-producing world with the knowledge that he can always scurry back to the safe haven provided by his mother when things get too scary.

In an ideal world, as the child gets a little older, he begins to form other bonds—for example, with his father at about age four, his immediate social environment at age seven, and the larger social environment at around age nine. By fifteen, a healthy child should feel safe within himself. But, as Chuck says, at that age many of us simply feel stranded and alone.

"Do you remember what it felt like to be fifteen?" he asked me between mouthfuls of French toast. "Highly disappointing, wasn't it?"

His point was that our dysfunctional social patterns break biologically compelled processes that could otherwise help us reach our potential. In our society, we interrupt even the earliest bonding experience between mother and child by administering drugs before childbirth, unnaturally encouraging labor to occur at certain times of day when more doctors are on duty, and immediately removing the newborn from the mother. Hospitals are practically designed to break this bond, Chuck said, beginning to get fired up. Sometimes the bond is even broken in utero, through the mother's diet or emotional state.

If that bond between mother and child is broken at any time, everything else goes south. Lacking a safe place to venture out from, a baby experiences anxiety instead of stress and loses many potential neuronal connections. What's worse, the brain periodically wipes out all unmilenated connections between neurons; the first such housecleaning occurs around age seven. Which explains why adults have about one-fifth the neuronal connections of a five-year-old, and which hints at how much of our early potential is lost through actual physical damage to the brain caused by a breakdown in the bonding process.

While our conversation seemed to be spinning farther and farther from golf, Chuck eventually looped back. As he helped himself to a few grapes and strawberries and a couple of pineapple slices from my plate, he explained that the way a healthy child explores outward from his safe place into the unknown world is through play. Play is nature's framework for learning. But if the child doesn't have an unconditionally bonded and secure place to run back to, he never feels fully safe to play.

Chuck believes that sports provide one of the best places for children to play and to develop healthy relationships with their parents. He cited such superathletes as Michael Jordan and Tiger Woods—who both enjoyed intensely close bonds with their fathers—to demonstrate what's possible when a child feels safe to play and explore. He emphasized that the freedom to play is the single most important factor related to performance—more than physical size, agility, or other influences. And he suggested that with a truly safe place to play from, anyone could accomplish anything.

"The human cell is boundless," he said. "When you call upon it, it will go farther. We don't have a fucking clue what the parameters are, and sports have proven that there are no limitations. Golfers, in particular, are Neanderthals in even appreciating that they have a brain, let alone knowing how to use it. Golfers impress me less than anyone alive. I'd like to see a golfer take a punch from George Foreman; then they'd have something to whine and complain about in sports."

I asked Chuck if he meant to imply that with the right parents and the complete safety to play I might have learned to shoot a basketball as well as Michael Jordan, despite my size and other apparent limitations. He replied that the human brain is more capable of miracles than anyone in our society acknowledges. Further, anything would have been possible if I'd wanted it enough and was truly safe to play as a child.

While I found it a little tough to accept that I could have won an NBA scoring title standing three inches short of six feet, I let this go—something you learn to do when spending a concentrated amount of time in the company of Chuck Hogan. He asks a lot of pointed questions to elicit assent with his views, and if you don't agree, he'll keep talking until you relent. This is part of his charismatic power: His own beliefs are so strong that you're willing to go along with him, at least conditionally, just to hear what follows.

Turning back to golf, Chuck concluded that because so many of us missed out on the natural bonding experience early in life—and therefore were never safe to play—and because, as a result, we may not possess ample neuronal connections to deal with changing conditions, many adults are still fully unable to "play" golf. The game is not simply a fun exploration, as games are meant to be. Instead, it involves judgment, analysis, criticism, metaphors, and implied meanings. For many players, score serves as a measure of self-esteem and golf is anything but play.

Leaning forward over his empty plate, Chuck looked me in the eye with great intensity and said, "The golf course is the safest environment imaginable. What in God's name could be safer? Yet people face more anxiety on golf courses—they're not just nervous, they're anxious—because they've never felt safe to just play. How far do we carry this insanity to think there could really be pressure in golf? You're just playing a game in the safest place around. How absurd is that, for godsakes?"

In addition to the fact that we may not have enjoyed a proper bonding experience as children, another problem hinders our ability to play in the present, as adults: our reliance on analysis. According to Hogan, even though biology has provided us with remarkable capacities, we often unwittingly suppress our potential by the way we use our brains. "We've become less natural and more intellectual," Chuck said.

As the breakfast crowd emptied out of the grill room and wandered off to prearranged tee times, Chuck explained that intellect is the part of the mind that asks whether something can be done, and then does it. But intelligence considers whether the action is really best for the entire organism. By relying on intellect, we make the mistake of focusing on content and results rather that processes— the exact reason why so many people find golf so frustrating. According to Hogan, "Golf has become a quest for 'mosts' and 'betters' in terms of clubs, techniques, and score. But it can be a game of process, learning, and growth. From these goals come the greatest performances."

He went on to say that our intelligence creates boundless potential, yet when that same intelligence causes us to experience something powerful that we don't understand—déjà vu, for example, or suddenly performing in the zone—we dress it up with religion or philosophy. "Eastern philosophy," Chuck posited, "is just dogma built around our natural intelligence. It makes religious what should simply be natural. We are so ill prepared for being in the zone that when it happens, we make up stuff to explain it. We take what should be purely natural and dress it up with fancy ideas. When our brains cause paranormal activity, we call it voodoo or religion, even in golf.

"And yet," Chuck continued, "we *are* smart. It's just that our talking, conventional, incredibly slow, stupid, *thinking* minds are too ego-bound to recognize, give reverence to, or let go to their brilliant subconsciouses."

Hogan finally concluded by admitting that we really can't talk about any of this because doing so engages that intellectual mind we need to escape from. What we need to do, according to Chuck, is to rediscover—beyond intellect and anxiety—how to safely and purely just play.

Which is part of what Chuck Hogan tries to teach. As we walked to his nearby office in the Golf Learning Center, he explained that his educational philosophy employs a humanities approach and draws on such diverse disciplines as Neuro-Linguistic Programming (NLP), Feldenkreis, Alexander Technique, kinesthesiology, education, technology, exercise physiology, quantum physics, and new and ancient traditions.

Chuck sees himself less as a golf instructor than as an educator, although he claims that studying education was most useful in showing him how not to teach. Like most alternative instructors, Chuck sees golf as a vehicle for communicating about far more important subjects—such as how to learn. When I asked him why he didn't stay in the field of education he said that as an educator you can't very well call the CEO of a major corporation and offer to teach him anything. He implied that as a golf guru, you could.

But Chuck claims that he is not a sports psychologist either, and he hates the words *teacher* and *lessons.* He insists that he doesn't have students, but "clients, or colearners." And he adds that he learns something working with every one of them, which allows him to continue doing what he does. He's also fond of admitting that the golf industry doesn't know quite how to characterize him.

As an educator, and based on his belief that all thinking is cultural thinking—that is, that we've reinforced our particular worldview through social institutions but have only incorporated one of many potential visions—Chuck advocates a rather unusual curriculum for our schools. He adamantly believes that children should be taught about healthy relationships, how to be good parents (to ensure that their children experience crucial bonding), and how to run a brain. He's even written a pamphlet on this last topic, titled *The Brain: A User's Manual*.

In terms of golf instruction, Hogan advocates intensive coaching on the front end—at least twelve sessions in which he can begin to help people get out of the way so that their amazing and seemingly unlimited brains can start to perform even a little more of what they're capable of.

In the midst of teaching a "colearner" how to play golf, Chuck may suddenly begin talking about virtually anything else at any moment—suggesting that we need to make birth a natural process again to really help people learn better, for example, but also providing antidotes for those of us who've already been born. For starters, he might suggest that we simply acknowledge, without guilt or blame, the mistakes made by our parents and ourselves, and try to correct these with our own offspring. Or he might recommend that we try to recover the bonds we lost as children, which will enable us to play without anxiety and threats to our self-esteem. He'll advocate bonding with ourselves, which involves allowing the heart cells and brain cells to operate in harmony, resulting in wisdom.

And he'll certainly demand that we learn how to play. When our activities are characterized by safety and humor and self-esteem, we'll begin to forge new neuronal connections and begin to grow. And this won't happen by thinking intellectually and working on the mechanics of such things as golf.

"Don't play sports to get somewhere," Chuck advised me. "There is nowhere to get. Sports should be played for the pure enjoyment of self, and because they're fun."

When we'd spent the entire morning talking over breakfast and in his spacious learning center office, my brain was exhausted. I decided I'd better go outside for a while and hit some golf balls on the practice range. Chuck refused to work with me on the range until I completed a few goal-setting tasks that he'd given me as homework, and when I asked if he had any advice for my practice session he waved one hand dismissively and said, "Just go play."

"How will I know if I'm just playing?" I asked.

"You'll have more energy coming off the range than when you go on. You'll have no idea how much time has passed. And you'll be laughing, giggling, snickering, squealing, and animating your body." As I started out the door, Chuck called after me. "If you really want to learn how to play," he added, "drive by a grade-school playground sometime and listen to the sounds. You'll know what play sounds like. You sure won't hear those sounds on a golf course, which is like a fucking library. To be in the men's club at a golf course you have to pound your clubs on the ground, and cuss and snarl, and then commiserate—and the root word of *commiserate* is *misery*—with the other members. Anyone who squeals or laughs or acts animated on the course can't be a member of the men's club. You'd be ostracized and excluded to a place that isn't safe. Pretty dumb, huh?"

Chuck smiled resignedly, signaling the end of our conversation. I headed out to the range.

It was an overcast day and the flags on the target greens snapped crisply in the wind. The range was empty and beautiful—rolling, grassy mounds, lush greens, and the mountains red in the desert distance.

I began by hitting seven-irons without thinking about mechanics, just watching the lovely trajectories and feeling the joy of the crisp, clean click of club on ball. I tried to vocalize—as Chuck had suggested—to really *feel* each shot, and joy rushed up in me. But I also felt fear and self-consciousness. And though I let out an occasional "yippee!" I also recognized that none of my actions was purely free. I was alone on the range, but it still felt as if I was being watched, judged. I didn't feel entirely safe to just let myself go, and I began to intellectualize this—to both think about what it meant and to ruminate on how I would write about the experience later on.

In *Magical Child,* Joseph Chilton Pearce explains, "Concern over survival, safety, or well-being immediately forces an evaluation of experience before the experience can take place. There is no unquestioned acceptance of the given, which is the hallmark of the whole child."

Pearce also says, "The compulsion to describe . . . is the very intervention that disrupts the performance which you desire and seek. You must come out of the trance to describe the trance. Language cannot communicate these things. . . . Words enforce separation between name and thing named."

Back at Esalen, Steve Cohen had asked us to return to a safe place in our minds, and I envisioned myself in the backyard of my childhood home on Long Island in the days before the peach tree got sick and had to be cut down. I was standing on the patio swatting a beach ball back and forth with my mother, and I felt absolutely safe and unconditionally loved. But I was very young then, and I can't remember having felt such an encompassing sense of safety since.

So over the years I adopted intellection as a means of protecting myself. I ultimately became a journalist, which allows me to stand outside even my own experience as a neutral observer. I have learned to disassociate from much of what happens in my life as a way of protecting myself from the pain potentially inflicted by an unsafe world, but in doing so I also shut out feelings of happiness, love, and joy. Even standing on the practice range on a perfectly lovely afternoon, I couldn't entirely enjoy myself without my intellectual mind standing guard.

After a morning with Chuck Hogan I understood that golf could help me along my path by providing an activity in which I could drop all intellection and analysis and learn to simply feel safe enough to play again. But to make any progress in golf—or in life—I'd finally have to fling my notebook over the cliff.

In the late afternoon, I stretched out on the giant bed in my hotel room and spent a couple of hours on the homework Chuck Hogan insisted I complete before we worked together on the practice range the following day. It was something he required of all his private and golf school students.

I started with an eleven-step process in which I was to list my golfing goals, prioritize them, visualize reaching them, develop a timeline, identify barriers to and resources supporting my goals, create an action plan, set subgoals, perform several other tasks, and then repeat the whole process.

I worked on this project well into the evening, as the light outside grew softer and then closed to darkness. While the desert wind kicked up, I wrote lists, crossed out goals, scribbled notes about the implications, and finally ended up with a very different set of priorities.

In describing how this process worked, Chuck had told me, "If you do this, you'll get to where you want to be. But ask for what you really want. Get extremely clear about it, and let it come to you. You can't get it by trying. Approaching it with a sense of ease sets the stage for feeling safe and getting what you want. There is no such thing as 'trying' in human experience. Trying is simply a way of stressing your system unnecessarily. Trying is absolute evidence that you are not doing what you wish."

Chuck had concluded our conversation about goals by saying, "We ask the wrong questions in golf, such as 'How can I get better, hit farther, and be more consistent?' The wrong questions lead us down the wrong path. We should ask: 'How can I be happier, and use golf instruction in my life?' We should ask: 'Since I have this magnificent brain designed to make me happy, how can I get out of the way so that it can do what it is elaborately designed to do with the greatest ease and grace?'"

Chuck had assured me—warned me, actually—that when you give the brain congruent instructions and step out of the way, everything works out for the best. He called this the basis of enlightenment.

If you're not getting what you desire, it means that your wants, beliefs, feelings, and behaviors are not in agreement.

"This gets bastardized and misunderstood," he'd said. "When a person is congruent he gets what he wants. Call it a miracle, but it's purely a biological process. What's a miracle is that we haven't learned this lesson. That's sad. People suffer humongously both psychologically and emotionally. We're all geniuses, but we refuse to open our minds. Which is a disease. A dis-ease."

Chuck also had me fill out several strange questionnaires meant to determine my hobbies, my golf history, and my ayurvedic body type—a system of classification used by various aboriginal cultures for the past fifty thousand years. Chuck would use these findings to further identify how to coach me, based partly on the kinds of sights, sounds, smells, sensations, and tastes I associated with a core state, or "being in the zone." If I were a PGA Tour player, he would also use the questionnaires to develop recommendations regarding my diet, daily schedule, seasonal schedule, practice routine, and other elements of care and feeding.

The following morning I met Chuck back in the grill room at the Raven, where he devoured another large breakfast while simultaneously noticing every single person who walked past, and greeting most of them by name. He was half distracted, yet completely engaged in our conversation, and even a little more playful and relaxed than he'd been yesterday. But no less intense. We spent an hour or so discussing my goal-setting homework and the various questionnaires I'd filled out, and then we finished eating and headed off to the learning center.

Even when we stood on the perfect grass of the practice range with my clubs beside us and a bucket of range balls spilling out in a tantalizing sweep, we spent much of my lesson talking. Or at least Chuck did.

He began by explaining the NLP concept of the model imperative, which suggests that all learning is based on modeling. But he made it clear that he was not talking about modeling the mechanics of someone else's golf swing. "Mechanical instruction is flat-ass out of its mind," he said, cutting to the chase. "It uses intellect—as opposed to intelligence—to dig an even deeper hole. If you focus successfully on the target, there are no mechanics, and if you're focusing on mechanics, you can't be aware of the target. You can't hit golf balls and work on mechanics at the same time."

Just as he began warming up to his subject, an errant golf ball flew toward us from a nearby fairway and came to a stop ten yards away on the practice tee. Chuck glanced up casually, as if someone had gently spoken his name. He looked at the ball and how far out of bounds it had landed. Then he followed the line of sight from this lie toward the green: It passed directly over—or through—the shiny glassed structure of the learning center offices.

"I'll bet the moron tries to hit it right over the building," Chuck said, shaking his head. Then he took the liberty of "improving" the player's OB lie in a way that discouraged such a shot.

Returning to the concept of the model imperative, Chuck described it as a process of perceiving something, repeating it, and developing a cycle of competence. The first step, called imprinting, occurs when you observe an action often enough for an image of it to imprint upon the mind. As an aside, he mentioned that when babies imprint walking, for example, it enhances their neuronal connections.

After imprinting an action, we must learn to repeat it. In addition to improving performance, repeating the imprinted action actually opens new gateways in the brain and milenates neuronal connections. Which is to say that even as adults, learning something new provides us with an opportunity to recapture some of our long-lost potential.

Our greatest problem in learning sports, however, is that early on many people learn to imprint a message that says "I can't," which can continue to hinder performance throughout our lives. If, for example, you had an older brother who found fault with all of your early athletic efforts, you might never shake that deeply imprinted message.

So when you take up fly fishing in your fifties, it's difficult to master the dry cast because a voice within you continues to whisper that you're no good and you'll never get it right.

In talking about our potential abilities—what we'd be able to accomplish if we heard no such negative messages—Chuck said, "We're not limited in sports by physical differences, but because of learning. Anything that one person can do another can do, too. Especially in golf, physical differences just don't matter very much."

After modeling and imprinting an action, the third step of the model imperative is habituation, by which you develop unconscious competence in the activity through positive association with correct repetitions. The fourth and final step is variation, by which you individualize the activity to better suit your own style and body type and make it your own.

Once you've developed competence in executing a skill, the biggest factor affecting performance is confidence, which depends mostly on whether you feel safe enough to really play whatever game you've been practicing. If you do feel safe—or, in other words, if you possesses both competence and confidence—there are no limits to what you can achieve. But since most of us missed out on having a natural and complete bonding experience early in life, anxiety more than likely causes us to feel unsafe. In particular, worrying about what other people might be thinking of us kills our performance in golf. Which is exactly what Fred Shoemaker had said back at Esalen.

Still, according to Chuck, if we accept the model imperative, acknowledge the baggage we've been dragging around since childhood, and negotiate with the "no" signals we've inherited (thereby halting the production of certain unhealthy chemicals), we can still grow and improve beyond many perceived limitations.

Of course, this entire learning process must be one of play, and with play there is no losing, no negativity. As Chuck said, "If you match your model, you must celebrate. If you don't match it, you must learn—like dart players do—how to close in on your goal. So the outcome is positive either way."

Chuck took a step back and pushed a single golf ball out in front of me with his foot. Finally, I thought. He instructed me to take out a seven-iron and hit a few shots. I grabbed the club and began to swing it easily, trying to loosen up.

Although I normally would have spent far more time stretching out and swinging the club to warm up, I stepped forward and addressed the ball that Chuck had nudged toward me.

I took a slow three-quarter backswing, made clean contact, and followed through to the finish. The ball sailed toward the 150-yard flag.

I looked at Chuck, at least aware that I sought his approval.

"Did you like it?" he asked.

I smiled, still admiring the shot. "It was pretty good."

Chuck stepped toward me and leaned his head even closer. Just as I expected him to whisper some advice or mild praise in his soft, disarming voice, he suddenly screamed, *"Yippee!"*

Which startled the hell out of me. I took a small step away from Chuck.

He pushed another ball out in front of me, and when my pulse began to settle back down, I stepped up and hit it. But I swung too fast and topped the shot into a bunker.

I turned to Chuck. "Not a very good one," I lamented, offering a sour face.

He said nothing, and set up another ball.

I hit this one well. We watched it fly high and draw slightly. "Woo-hoo!" he screamed. "Woo-hoo!" He stared at me in a way meant to encourage my participation. He put his hands up for high-fives and I slapped them awkwardly.

I laughed, waiting for him to set up another ball, but Chuck engaged me with a very serious look, his brows practically making tunnels of his eyes.

He explained that the best advice he could offer me was to "associate" with my good shots by yelling and jumping up and down and really emoting. Conversely, he recommended that I "disassociate" from my bad shots, simply noticing them without lending them any emotional content that might cause me to imprint or remember them. I should register awareness of bad shots, and say only, "Isn't that interesting."

"You can't moderate your emotions, but you can disassociate from the bad ones," Chuck told me. "I'm always amazed when I see a golfer who won't express 'yippee skippee,' or other behaviors that indicate joy and satisfaction—a guy who watches a positive outcome with surprise or neutrality, but when he gets an inappropriate outcome he grimaces, frowns, curses, slams his clubs, or uses tonalities in his voice. These knee-jerk responses are stored in the memory banks, and they're very unhealthy."

So I hit a few more balls and tried to follow Chuck's advice. When my shots felt pure and traveled high and long, I squeaked out a few halfhearted "yippees," all the while self-conscious about what the other golfers around might think if I got so excited about a seven-iron shot on the practice range. Which reinforced Chuck's point that I did not feel safe to play.

In concluding this part of my "lesson," Chuck reiterated that I had learned to disassociate and to deaden my voice. I recognized that I'd done this as a way of protecting myself, and I also knew that more recently, I'd concluded that disassociating (or simply not feeling things) is a bad pattern I needed to break out of. But Chuck's advice was that I simply need to use this skill more selectively, so I associate more fully to feel everything from the emotion of lovemaking to the thrill of hitting a great golf shot—thereby imprinting such feelings—but disassociate from anxiety, negative messages, and bad golf shots.

Chuck's final advice about associating carried the concept into my practice regimen. He recommended that after every round of golf and every practice session I take a few moments to reflect on the shots I'd hit. Starting with generalities, I should begin to see, feel, hear, touch, and taste the sensations that each shot produced. As he put it, I should move from superfluff to fluff to very precise images. For example, if my good shots seemed to suggest the color blue, I should determine that it was a dark blue and explore this fully enough to recognize that it was the rich color of the cover of my history notebook in college. If I noticed a sweet banana smell in connection with a perfect three-iron to the green, I should hone that scent to the exact one that reminded me of a certain beach house I'd stayed in for a week on the island of Bonaire. He suggested that I use precise language in associating with these specifics and try to call up positive associations as often as possible. I should image the perfect flight of a golf ball in the same way that, if I was in love, I would see the image of my lover all the time. And he encouraged me to emote—to moan, whisper, coo, and croon—every time I succeeded. Because everything that you make real begins as an image, and associating with positive images is essential to getting in the zone.

Over the next hour or so, Chuck and I worked more specifically on my golf swing, but that was far less interesting than hearing about how I should vocalize during lovemaking. For starters, Chuck didn't like the way that all my divots pointed to the left, so he tried to get me to swing farther outside and turn my hands over. He eventually brought out a long cardboard box from his office and set it up just outside the ball, angling away from me, then had me practice swinging the club along the line of the box. We worked on this until I imprinted a model for a new swing.

Chuck "yippeed" each time I got it right, and recommended that I practice this in the mirror at least sixty times every night for at least three weeks, yippeeing whenever I matched the model, and observing "Isn't that interesting" when I didn't. When I was confident that I'd learned the correct swing, I should continue repeating it until it was habituated. Then I could first think about addressing an actual golf ball—but without focusing on a target. I should just observe the ball's flight, which should be high and slightly right to left. When I could habitually make the ball move that way I could begin aiming at something. This process would take me anywhere from three weeks to five months.

But Chuck also suggested that to cut my handicap in half I avoid even going to the range or hitting golf balls or practicing on the putting green. Instead, I should simply putt indoors with a putting track made of two-by-fours, practicing aim and alignment so as to learn whether my habitual aim is accurate, randomly inaccurate, or consistently inaccurate. Once I knew this, I could calibrate it to be more consistently accurate. Accomplishing that, I should then focus all my attention on distance response by putting on an actual green. But I should strike every other ball with my eyes closed to develop a true feel for distance.

Finally, I needed to work on my short game from ninety yards in, using my new swing. Although my old stroke would prove effective on short shots, using it would erode my better and recently mastered stroke.

How I went about learning all of this would be the critical issue. The content was irrelevant, but the process was immeasurably important. I *must* celebrate the good and disassociate from the negative.

"The whole thing is to live in joy," Chuck concluded. "You can read self-help books, pursue years of therapy, NLP, Gestalt, et cetera. Or you can say 'I'm going to choose to be happy. I'll never turn my back on it.' Then to match your behavior to that is the whole damned thing. This is where golf instruction is so fucked up. It keeps talking about how it's hard work. It's not. It's deep play, but it takes discipline because the entire adult community refuses to do it. We're so estranged we won't even let our own kids do it."

And, he said, this applied to absolutely everything. "Golf is not like life. Golf is life."

3

Heartland Golf School:

Fantastic Voyage in Search of the Authentic Swing

The game of golf is not confined to a board or a court or even a field. Golf is large as life. As in life, we stand alone on the tee with no opponent and no teammate. It is us for ourselves and sometimes against ourselves. We stand alone with the ball and our dream.　　　　—ED LeBEAU

ED LEBEAU'S YOUNG son had an excruciatingly painful earache, so Ed encouraged him to go inside his ear to see what was up in there. The boy looked at him strangely.

LeBeau just shrugged.

"Maybe I could unscrew the outer part of my ear and go in that way?" his son said.

"That might work."

Bingo. Once inside, the boy saw a very small room and heard a voice, yelling.

"What's the voice saying?" Ed asked.

"'It's too small in here!'"

"What does it want?"

"More room!"

"Will the room grow bigger?"

"Okay," his son said.

"Is that good enough for the voice?"

"I think so."

When he came back out of his own ear, the boy's pain had abated.

Similarly, a friend of Ed's—an eighty-year-old doctor of psychology—was having some trouble with his prostate. So the man unscrewed his ear, entered his own body, and snaked down past ribs and internal organs toward the delicate part in question. Arriving there, he saw an eight-inch balloon with a cork stuck in the end. After removing the cork, he immediately felt less pressure. Ed's friend also claims to have cured his arthritis through this process, known as "inner guided imagery." It differs from the kind of guided visualization that Steve Cohen conducted at Esalen by venturing largely through territory within the body and mind. Still, throughout my journey to various alternative golf schools, I was struck by similarities such as this one as much as by differences in approach. Such similarities lend credence to the notion that genuine truths often evolve simultaneously in distinct and dispersed cultures that have no contact with each other—the same way that certain aspects of toolmaking appeared simultaneously in early human cultures separated by entire continents.

At a time when many golf instructors have broken down the swing to a molecular level and employ video cameras, computer modeling, and radar guns to analyze and correct mechanics, Ed LeBeau has taken a different tack. He employs this particular type of creative visualizing to treat the golfing ills of students at his Heartland Golf Schools.

I attended a two-and-a-half-day school in August, when St. Louis was hot and wet as an old work glove and overrun by a hundred thousand Baptists in town for a convention. On the first morning of the workshop at the Annbriar Golf Club, LeBeau asked our class of three students to imagine we'd videotaped our last three rounds of golf, watched the tapes, and chosen the best six drives, approaches, and putts from those rounds, then strung those shots together. "Wouldn't that make for the kind of golf you've always dreamed of playing," he mused. LeBeau theorized that golfers don't need to learn anything new about the swing, or to practice mechanics, because somewhere inside we already know how to hit great shots: The proof is that we've already done it.

"A golf swing is a lot like handwriting," Ed said that first morning. "You have to stay with your own instead of copying someone else's. Our goal is not to change any of your swing mechanics, but rather to help you find your own mechanics and the swing that already works for you. While the physics involved in effectively launching a golf ball is the same for all players, how each of us learns and triggers our swing is different." Ed suggested that when we could consistently execute the swing that had led to our best shots in the past, we'd get into the zone and play much better golf—the golf we were capable of playing.

Ed borrowed aspects of this theory from a novel called *The Legend of Bagger Vance,* by Stephen Pressfield. In the novel, a mystical golf caddie expresses the idea that we each possess an "Authentic Swing" that is unique to us. To try to learn another swing—such as one taught by a professional golf instructor, or modeled after Tiger Woods, for example (especially one modeled after Tiger Woods)— only leads us farther away from our true selves.

As Pressfield writes, ". . . our task as golfers is simply to chip away all that is inauthentic, allowing our Authentic Swing to emerge in its purity. . . . In this line of discussion, we could equate the swing with the soul, the Authentic Soul or the Authentic Self. This is the reason for the endless fascination of golf. The game is a metaphor for the soul's search for its true ground and identity—self-realization.

"The search for the Authentic Swing is parallel to the search for the Self. We as golfers pursue that elusive essence our entire lives. What hooks us about the game is that it gives us glimpses . . . of our

Authentic Swing. . . . All we need is to experience . . . one mid-iron screaming like a bullet toward the flag, one driver flushed down the middle—and we're enslaved forever. We feel with absolute certainty that if we could only swing like that all the time, we would be our best selves, our true selves, our Authentic Selves."

Bagger Vance spends much of the book delivering diatribes on how a player can access his Authentic Swing by passing from pre-consciousness to self-consciousness to enlightenment. According to Vance, there are three possible paths to follow:

1. Discipline, which involves beating zillions of range balls and ultimately ends in defeat when the player surrenders.

2. Wisdom, which involves analysis, dissection, and other mental processes, but results in paralysis because the brain eventually shuts down.

3. Love, the true path to enlightenment, by which learning occurs through childlike reverence and passion.

Bagger Vance's notion of the Authentic Swing is not that different from Fred Shoemaker's notion of the Original Swing, except in one aspect. Fred made it very clear that he was not offering us enlightenment. In fact, when I asked him about this one day at Esalen, he asked me how we could even talk about enlightenment when neither of us really had any idea what it was. "Whatever you think it is," Fred had told me, "I can guarantee you that it's not that."

Whether it offers a path toward enlightenment or not, discovering our authentic or original swings provides a worthy goal for golf. And Ed LeBeau believes that the best way to find this swing is by exploring our interior rather than fixating on the swing's exterior manifestation. Which is to say by going inside. At the same time, his methods provide a means of visiting our own prostates, should that ever become desirable.

LeBeau is a handsome cross between Bob Eubanks from the old *Newlywed Game* and Corbin Bernsen, who played Arnie on *L.A. Law*. His ravenous curiosity is only surpassed by the breadth of his reading and the frightening sound of his strange laugh. He talks easily about everything from *Star Wars* to Sufism, tai chi to the Catholic Church in the time it takes to blow out a puff of stogie. He founded Heartland Golf Schools after retiring at age forty-six. For folks who are tired of pounding range balls and sick to death of hearing tall, skinny PGA guys yammering on about weak grips and reverse pivots, the school's methods provide a welcome respite.

The Chinese Taoist concept of Wu Wei, LeBeau told us that first morning, counsels that visualization produces a desired result more often than the ego's desire or the brain's knowledge can. Much of the inner guided imagery that we practiced at Heartland was aimed at honing our abilities to visualize not only great golf shots, but also aspects of our own character that would help make them possible. While the school's curriculum acknowledges the importance of the external (including such swing fundamentals as grip, stance, and posture), it focuses on the internal performance fundamentals that determine how much of our swing's potential we'll realize.

As Ed continued his opening remarks by talking about how we play our best golf from the subconscious, I noticed two of my classmates—a large couple who'd only recently taken up golf—glancing at each other like teenagers sharing a joke about their high-school teacher. They were eager to play golf and skeptical about this new-age golf instruction not focused around pounding golf balls.

By the time Ed finished talking about visualization, my fellow students appeared as if they might implode. When he talked about awareness I'm not certain they were even listening anymore—a beautiful paradox. They were staring longingly at the lovely Annbriar Golf Course beyond the window of the conference room. Perhaps they were visualizing themselves hitting tight approaches that stuck close to the pin.

Although much of what Ed talked about was already familiar to me, I liked the way he presented the concepts. In talking about awareness, he described how in the martial arts, good body strength defeats poor body strength, good technique defeats good body strength, and good presence defeats good technique. He defined presence as "active awareness"—which he had plenty of.

For the entirety of my Heartland experience we spent a fair amount of time going inside to explore "whole-brain golf," in which the hemispheres of our brain are supposed to work together to help us live up to our potential. Ed began by having us close our eyes, and then he led a guided imagery as if he was the captain of some inner spacecraft embarked upon a fantastic journey through our own bodies and minds. In a calm, deep voice he asked us to imagine that we were in the center of our head. "Spend a little time there," he encouraged; "notice what it's like." Following each exploratory mission to new territory, we'd come back out and report on the geography of where we'd been.

That first morning our excursions took us to the separate hemispheres of our brain, where Ed encouraged us to venture forth and hit a few golf shots. We would begin to build our golf games from there, drawing on the best that each hemisphere could provide. I experienced a sense of power and control in my right hemisphere, but my left felt like unfamiliar territory. It was like a back bedroom that I wandered into every now and then looking for a shirt or an old sweater, but I never settled in there to spend any quality time.

Next, we visited imaginary golf courses on each side and then one in the center, noticing the differences between them and considering what those differences might mean. For example, my right-hemisphere golf course appeared all lush and manicured, while my left-hemisphere layout was covered in brown grass dappled with barren spots, suggesting that I don't spend much time cultivating my left side, and might benefit from residing in that hemisphere a little more. My integrated-brain golf course was a challenging combination of the Woodlands—a resort course in Texas featuring plenty of water shaped by sleek wooden bulkheads—and the rollicking mounds of the TPC Stadium Course at Sawgrass, in Ponte Vedra Beach, Florida. Just looking at this wonderful design floated joy and exhilaration up in me like bubbles rising in a glass of champagne.

For our next task, Ed asked us to hit golf balls from the intersection of three lines in our head, and have a peek at our crown chakras while we were at it. Considering this power spot atop my head, I saw a palm tree set against a deep blue Caribbean sky. When Ed asked me what this meant, I responded, "It could provide rootedness. It's tall and it grows in sand, which is a metaphor for making the most out of little—an apt description of my entire athletic career."

We visited our earth centers and heart centers and hit a few shots. We dropped by the solar plexus center. Eventually LeBeau asked us to visualize ourselves playing each shot on several holes of an imaginary golf course. If we shanked or dribbled, we should turn to our "inner golf pro" who always walks the course with us, to ask his opinion of what we'd done wrong.

My first imaginary hole was a par-four dogleg left somewhere in Florida, with white shell-lined bunkers and grand white hotels looming in the blue distance. I drew my tee shot into the dogleg and watched it land and bounce perfectly on the flat fairway. Then I hit an eight-iron 150 yards to the green and sank my putt for birdie.

The second hole was a par five that curved left around a lake. The deep, lush, green verticut fairways reminded me of a hole on the wonderful Crosswater Golf Course in the high desert of central Oregon. My huge honkin' drive landed parallel to a bunker in the middle of the fairway—a daring and well-executed poke. For my second shot, I swung right out of my orthotics with a three-wood and slightly faded the ball into the first cut of rough just short and to the right of the green. I turned and consulted my inner golf pro, who was actually toting my bag. His name was Connery, and he looked a lot like my conception of Shivas Irons in *Golf in the*

Kingdom—a grizzled, white-haired wild man with gnarled hands. I felt great comfort in knowing that he'd come along just to help me when I needed him. Connery admitted that it wasn't a bad shot, but that it might have faded because I didn't complete my follow-through. He spoke with a whiskey-rough Scottish brogue I could barely understand.

Walking up to the ball, I considered the very tough approach I'd left myself over a couple of gaping bunkers to a small, slopey green. I asked Connery for a sand wedge and then lofted a solid pitch high above two traps and onto the bent grass green. I knocked my double-breaking lag putt close enough to tap in for par. *Aaargh!* we roared in stereophonic triumph—oddly, like pirates.

The third imaginary hole was a 230-yard par three over a deep ravine and malevolent bunkers. I hit a low-trajectory shot into the very front of the slope leading up to the green, and it rolled up to the fringe. I two-putted for another par.

I obviously excelled at visualized golf, and wondered whether I should visualize a gallery full of admiring fans who might buy me visualized drinks in the imaginary clubhouse. I'm not entirely certain what the point of this exercise was, but both Connery and I enjoyed it immensely. Perhaps LeBeau had designed it to help us experience the feeling of playing perfect golf, or to make this kind of play more likely after we'd visualized it, as Wu Wei implied. When I asked him about this Ed responded, "We can learn faster and more in depth from seeing something than we can from a verbal description of it. Like with riding a bicycle. Visualization is an accelerated and more powerful way of learning. That's why it's helpful to see ourselves making a great golf swing."

As we talked about our experiences, I was surprised to hear that none of my classmates played very well even though the outcome was completely within their control.

We finished that first morning out on the putting green in heat that pressed down upon us with amazing force. Although Ed encouraged us to try to let our Authentic Swings come out, he also engineered how we were supposed to putt, and I resented the intrusion upon my own processes. I'd already developed a successful method for climbing out of consciousness and into the zone while putting, and it had worked well thanks to the awareness drills I'd practiced at Esalen.

When I mentioned my difficulty to Ed, he said he'd certainly think about what I was saying. But he also said that you can't fill a bucket with fresh water until you empty it first—a subtle suggestion that I let go of what I'd been doing and simply try his method.

Watching the other students putting, I wondered what might happen if the swing you visualized wasn't a good one. It was obviously time for lunch and an afternoon off.

On our second morning Ed delivered a short talk on power. He observed that when we push a broom, or move a refrigerator, or even pull on a garden hose, our power emanates from a spot behind our navels. He asked us to close our eyes for a moment, and as we settled back and breathed deeply into a state of relaxation, he *slammed* a book on the table in front of us and we all felt that sudden surge of adrenaline in our midsections. Ed explained that when we feel fear—in approaching a golf shot, or in any other situation—our power center rises up, but by breathing deeply we can settle the power back to the center so we're free to swing the golf club from that place.

To further demonstrate how fear and tension sap energy from a shot, Ed handed us each a tennis ball and asked us to squeeze it tightly. While we were squeezing, he asked us to toss the ball at a garbage can a few feet away. All our shots fell short of the target.

But when we repeated the exercise with light grips, our shots sailed over the can, demonstrating that flexibility, and not tension, is an important aspect of power.

Today the weather had cleared, and though it was still hot, the sky was a rich summer blue. In the late morning we went outside to practice on the chipping green. I tried to feel my Authentic Swing and focused on my breath. I inhaled deeply while addressing each shot, and then exhaled to release tension and return to my power center. Then I imagined the feel of a well-struck shot and let go. Ed had set a plastic drink cup in the middle of the green as a target, and I knocked it over half a dozen times.

At lunch, we watched foursomes of golfers playing out around the eighth green just outside the window of the clubhouse restaurant. Between bites of his cheeseburger, my classmate Chuck leaned toward me and whispered that he wished we'd go out and play some "real golf."

But in the afternoon we only ventured as far as the driving range. Ed placed a bucket of balls about twenty yards behind each of us so that we'd have to slow our pace by walking back to retrieve a ball between each shot rather than quickly pounding the whole bucket out at the target in no time flat.

When we worked on air-lifting shots to a flag fluttering about seventy-five yards away, my wedges all flew the green by a good twenty yards. I was already using my most lofted club, so I couldn't hit less stick. Ed suggested that I ask my inner pro for advice.

"Connery recommends a flop shot," I said.

"Okay."

"I don't know how to hit a flop shot."

"Can you ask him?"

We consulted. Connery mumbled a Scottish epitaph. "He doesn't really know, either," I reported.

Ed considered this a moment, as if such a possibility hadn't occurred to him.

"Why don't you experiment a little."

So I tried to hit flop shots without consciously wondering how to do so. But the balls continued to rocket over the green.

When I summoned Ed back over for further consultation, he suggested that I venture inside my "control room." I opened an imaginary door and stepped into a small space full of cables and computers, where a bunch of technicians sat in front of a wall of monitors.

"Talk to them," Ed suggested.

The head technician was a fat guy named Murray who was top-less and sporting a chest tattoo that read, MY FRIENDS VISITED JEFF'S BRAIN AND ALL I GOT WAS THIS LOUSY INK. I asked Murray what I should do about my wedge shots traveling too far.

"You need to let go more," Murray advised in a Brooklyn accent. He slapped a palm to his forehead. "Duh-uh."

In response, I gave the entire control room staff the rest of the day off, which proved extremely liberating and allowed me to play golf without worrying about what I was accomplishing. I never quite solved the flop-shot problem, but figured that it would work itself out over time.

Later that afternoon, while hitting some shots on the practice range, I experienced an insight related to those thoughts about writ-ing that had occurred to me at Esalen. As I floated a string of seven-irons at a practice green, I realized that by becoming a writer, I'd chosen the perfect activity for harmonizing the two hemispheres of my brain.

In writing—an activity I usually managed to perform without self-consciousness—the creative, free-flowing, and emotional side of my brain could generate wild ideas and deep feelings, but to actual-ly write about them coherently I also relied on the analytical, struc-tured, grammar-producing hemisphere. I'm not sure what this had to do with golf except that it occurred to me while rattling off a series of perfect seven-irons. I thought about what Chuck Hogan had said about letting go of the intellectual approach and recognized that maybe I didn't have to give it up entirely—I just needed to use it more selectively.

On our final morning at Heartland we actually went out to play golf—nine holes that took more than three hours. My greatest accomplishment of the day was remaining calm and patient and playing well despite the gruelingly slow pace of my classmates. Even when I took a nine on one hole, I refrained from falling into the sinkhole of anger and self-consciousness. I actually hit each of those nine shots well: My drive ended up on a side slope and I overcompensated for the lie and crushed a three-wood that did not fall off nearly as much as I expected it to, and so it disappeared into the woods. So I dropped and struck another perfect shot that went so far down the middle of the fairway that it trickled into a creek I hadn't thought I'd be able to reach. I laughed at my predicament as my classmates hacked and chunked their way up the lovely fairways.

After golf, and following lunch, Ed LeBeau asked us to consult one more time with our inner golf pro to discover what he had to offer us to take away from the school. Connery told me it was time to stop working so hard on my swing and just *play* the game more fully. I suspected he'd been talking to Murray in the control room, and possibly to Chuck Hogan. I knew they were all right, but it would take me a long time to really be able to heed their advice.

Ed LeBeau prepared us for our golfing futures with a short talk about mastery. He suggested that the paradox surrounding mastery was that we could only achieve it through surrender; when we try to conquer the golf course, it drains our energy, and we're the ones who get conquered. It wasn't a novel idea—the notion of letting go has become almost a cliché in golfing circles. But LeBeau explained it in a way that made perfect sense.

He said there were two ways you could shoot a seventy-three: There is the seventy-three of surrender, where electricity flows through your body and the game energizes you; and there's the grinding, sweaty seventy-three of willpower. You might expect to see the guy who shot the seventy-three of willpower drinking too much and smoking in the clubhouse bar before returning home to his third wife.

As a final stop on our inner guided imagery tour, Ed asked us to close our eyes and imagine a place that was special to us. I pictured a lovely, wild stretch of the Salmon River, in Idaho, where I work for part of each summer as a whitewater river guide. In my visualization, the clear green river cascaded over and around boulders and rounded stones. The sun shone on the water, and ponderosa pines receded gently up the banks.

Asked to make room for a golf shot in my image, I visualized a green floating on the calm water above the rapid. I stroked a high eight-iron from a sandy beach, and when my ball landed on the putting surface, the river swept it back down to me, completing a circle and filling me with power and ease.

"As you change your approach to the game of golf, you begin to attend," Ed LeBeau told us in final benediction. "But you cannot and will not confine your learning to the golf course. Soon, you'll find that you're beginning to change your approach and are better attending to the rest of your life. By changing the person you are on the golf course, you change the person you are with your spouse. Improved patience, creative vision, and personal reflection can and will show up at home and in your workplace. By changing your golf, you put yourself on the road to changing your life. How's that for a reason to get rid of your slice?"

4

On the Edge:
Adventures in . . . Golf?

. . . Life is nothing but a series of fascinations, an odyssey from world to world. And so with golf. An odyssey it is—from hole to hole, adventure after adventure, comic and tragic, spellin' out the human drama.
—Shivas Irons, in Michael Murphy's *Golf in the Kingdom*

Eighteen of us—mostly men—were sitting around in the Sturgeon Bay Room at the American Club Resort in Kohler, Wisconsin. Close by, four of the world's most beautiful and daunting golf courses lounged like supermodels, but we were confined to this conference room. We'd been asked by Steve Cohen, my old friend from Esalen, to write our own conclusions to a sentence that began: "One thing I've always wanted to do but have been afraid to do is ____." As pens scratched on legal pads, I considered how I've avoided rowing a boat through the Grand Canyon on the Colorado River, visiting India, or climbing above twenty thousand feet. I thought of other enticing adventures that spooked the bejesus out of me.

When we'd had ample time to scribble our confessions, Cohen asked us to share what we'd written—which could have proved scarier than the things we were admitting frightened us. A well-groomed man in crisp khakis volunteered to go first. He earnestly told the group that one thing he'd always wanted to do but had been afraid to do was develop an effective business plan.

In the spirit of Iron John, new-age acceptance, and all that hoo-ha, I struggled not to judge him, or to act smug. But I was sorely tempted to leap across the circle and beat the crap out of this perfectly nice man.

As I further considered how I'd explain my own biggest fear (commitment—duh!), a forty-seven-year-old financial adviser named John Shaffer cleared his throat across the circle, indicating that he was ready to reveal what he was afraid to do. Shaffer was built like a packing crate, but his guttural Pennsylvania accent and tough expression belied a certain tenderness, I intuited.

"Go to a whorehouse," Shaffer said.

Adventure is commonly measured by daring feats and dangerous risks, and almost always involves some degree of fear. But it's good to remember that various folks are afraid of heights or water, grizzly bear attacks, dental checkups, tainted sushi, or even business plans. Despite the many differences between us, our group of eighteen had gathered for an adventurous weekend at the American Club because what we shared, in part, was a fear of golf. We had traveled from as far away as Hawaii, New York, and Oregon to participate in this workshop called Golfing on the Edge.

Run by the Shivas Irons Society (named after the golf pro in *Golf in the Kingdom*), this long weekend was meant to provide a jumping-off point—literally—for an exploration of the landscape of fear and the topography of risk, not to mention the phobia of flop shots. It was about coming to terms with how being afraid adversely affects our performance not only in golf, but in other sports, business, relationships, and a thousand other aspects of life that can prove adventurous. Specifically, the weekend combined discussion groups, guided visualizations, interactive exercises, and—the real attraction for me—a high ropes course experience. Oh yes, and there would be rounds of golf on two of the American Club's gnarly world-class venues.

Our teachers at Golfing on the Edge included Cohen, the therapist; Steve Proudman, the adventure guy; and Andy Nusbaum, whom I also met at Esalen. All three were what you might call adventure philosophers. Proudman was a former Outward Bound instructor who uses adventure activities to teach corporate workshops. With a goatee just beginning to show gray, he exuded hipness and calm in equal measures. He was a man you'd be happy to have belaying you. Talking about adventure in philosophical terms, he said, "Adventures can happen anywhere. What defines an adventure is different for each individual." Which is to say, some of us orienteer or heli-ski for our excitement; others chip and pitch and putt.

While he agreed that adventures generally involve risk—whether physical or emotional—and often fear, Proudman thought a few other essential elements were also requisite. "An adventure is a place where your spirit plays in ways that are new and different, and where the outcome is not predetermined," he said. "It can be a great meal, or anything you're trying for the first time. Learning takes place around the experience, whether while the adventure is happening, or later. And any adventure is a process of self-discovery."

So let us consider actual adventures for a moment. Fact is that although I have bagged my share of mountain peaks, guided whitewater river trips, nearly been killed twice while scuba diving, and performed the requisite number of dumb stunts involving drugs, cars, and sometimes both, as an avid golfer I have experienced nearly equal amounts of fear on the cushy green haven of the golf course, and it has compromised my potential. How silly is that?

I journeyed to Kohler in hopes of discovering what was wrong with me and finding a way to fix it. Recognizing that fear has also held me back, for example, in my romantic involvements, I was willing to try anything—even treating golf as an adventure sport—to break through. As Andy Nusbaum liked to remind us, "If you do the same things you always do, you'll get the same results you always get."

Steve Proudman, no weenie himself, could relate to the deeper challenges I've experienced on the golf course. He admitted, "For me, golf has become an adventure experience because the ball doesn't do what I want it to, and that brings up a lot of control issues."

Okay, wait a sec. Clearly the golfer confronting a long three-iron shot over water to a two-tiered green during his club championship does not face the same kind of danger that stares down a kayaker paddling into a Class V drop. And when golfers refer to "hazards" they often mean shallow, man-made ponds covered in green scum and duck poo.

Yet in terms of their emotions—and the chemical reactions causing those emotions—the golfer and the kayaker may be having very similar experiences. Fear ekes out its scrappy existence in the brain, not in the environment, and those cranky cousins—fear and risk—often conspire to limit our performance in whatever we're afraid of, whether the risks are actual or metaphorical: in effect, anywhere that even something as minor as a lost Titleist is at stake.

Sure, there's a certain amount of humor implicit in the idea of confronting fear and having an adventure through golf. But there's something poignant at work here, too. In fact, the true heart of adventure palpates every time you step up to the tee while any number of variables—fear of failure or loss of control, worries that your partners won't like you or will think you weak if you chunk a sleeve of balls into the shrubbery, dread that your lover might desert you, distracting thoughts of a cheeseburger and a cold beer—threaten to impede your performance. Because it's a static sport (no maniacal defenders, no fast-moving pucks or balls), golf provides an ideal training ground, a perfect metaphor for learning how to perform with grace under pressure and to act rather than react. Like a ropes course or belayed climbing, it's also a safe laboratory for learning to manage fear: You can play the game without ever worrying about packing out the broken bodies of your friends if they have a bad day.

If you're someone who really cares about performing well, the adventure is heightened; and in riskier pursuits, your life may depend on executing well under these or larger pressures. The notion of golf as an adventure into the realms of fear and risk—even if that risk is that a downhill putt for birdie, which you desperately want, may roll off the green—takes on even greater import when you realize that far more people are likely to face these kinds of challenges in a pair of Dockers and a polo shirt on the golf course than hanging from a bivvy bag on the windblown face of the Eiger.

During our first afternoon at Golfing on the Edge, we stumbled monsterlike around our conference room with our eyes closed, walked an actual golf hole in silence, drew crayon pictures of our "safe place," screamed primally, and held hands, among other things. Some of this was familiar to me from Esalen, some new. I felt open and hopeful, if also skeptical and a little reserved. I was waiting for the real adventure, which began the next morning on the American Club's Team Challenge Course.

The first of our two challenges was to inch forty feet up a mostly vertical climbing wall to a platform, and then descend on a wild yee-haw ride via a zip line hung from a long cable. Everyone who tried climbing the wall made it up with more or less grace, with varying degrees of sewing-machine leg. Several decided not to try at all, and no one cajoled them. John "Whorehouse" Shaffer, compact and intense, scurried up the surface like Spiderman on black beauties, as if he could outclimb fear.

When we all finished with the wall, Steve Proudman introduced us to our second challenge, called the Pamper Pole because you might have benefited from wearing that item of infant couture while ascending forty feet up the pole—although you were belayed on two separate safety lines. The pole was essentially a giant vertical toothpick with a tiny platform perched on top.

John Shaffer and I were assigned as partners to scramble up the pole together. I climbed first and managed to stand atop the platform on wobbly legs. Below, the ground looked like a sixteen-millimeter film shot with an unstable camera. Shaffer scampered up behind me with a determined look, his mustache quivering slightly, and straddled the platform because there was barely room for one of us to stand. A moment later, the scariest part of the weekend occurred for Shaffer. As I prepared to launch myself off the platform toward a trapeze hanging from a cable ten feet away, I maintained my balance by resting a hand on Shaffer's climbing helmet. As my partner confessed to me later, "I thought, *Oh, my God. Is my head going with you?*"

We both completed our leaps, but were followed by only a couple of other participants still wishing to challenge themselves further. After jumping from atop the pole and being lowered back to earth, a fellow named Stan swore that he'd never sweat a difficult golf shot again in his natural life. For most of the others in our group, however, the climbing wall had provided enough adventure for one morning. Shaffer and Stan and I were all exhilarated by our experience. But one essential and now familiar question remained—as it often seems to in alternative golf schools: What could this possibly have to do with golf?

That afternoon, we played the American Club's River Course at the Blackwolf Run golf complex. Ranked among the toughest golf venues in the United States, the River Course is long, brutal, unforgiving, and beautifully designed. Water comes into play on twelve holes, and the holes themselves carry names like Gotcha, Hell's Gate, and Blind Alley. Three of us in my foursome were still pumped up from the morning, during which we overcame our fear and enjoyed the rush of an adventure well met. We believed we were ready for anything, and decided to play the River Course from the rather distant and difficult blue tees. Steve Heller, a fifty-nine-year-old retired entrepreneur who had decided against climbing or jumping off anything high at the ropes course, chose the shorter, easier white tees despite the implied peer pressure to be daring adventurers like the rest of us. Which in its own way constituted a brave stance.

On the front nine alone, I launched seven golf balls into the water, hit several innocent and unsuspecting trees, and blasted in—and still in—and eventually out of three sand traps. On the eighth hole, which stretched 512 yards, I earned a score so high that I simply entered an X on my scorecard and practiced looking sheepish. As we approached the tenth tee box, the rest of us joined Steve Heller on the white (read: pussy-boy) tees.

On the sixteenth hole—540 yards of mayhem, sand traps, and river—I actually flubbed two shots that I could have kicked farther, something I've hardly done since I was twelve years old. I decided to stop keeping score. Now I'd had enough adventure for one afternoon. Jumping off that damned pole seemed easy compared to playing bad golf, and I wondered if that was somehow the point. I was deeply disappointed that my successful adventure hadn't translated to improved performance. At least I maintained my sense of humor: I didn't blow up at anyone, or throw my clubs, as I've seen many golfers do when they're not up to the challenge at hand.

John Shaffer (a single-digit handicap) played in another foursome on the River Course that afternoon but reported a similar experience. He later reflected that the ropes course "probably made me less careful on the golf course. I probably had eight strokes I shouldn't have had—like where I hit two in the water on one hole because I had no fear: I had just overcome it all, and that numbed me from being sane. On another hole I tried to cut a corner and hit three more in the water. It was like that scene at the end of the movie *Tin Cup.*"

But Shaffer believed there was an upside to his careless play and high score. "It would have been easy to go for the safe side of the fairway, but then I'd have lived with regret and wondered whether I could've made it across the water. My score suffered, but I don't have to wonder. The payoff was to not fear failure, and to know that the consequences were not life threatening, nothing was going to change other than my score, and that wasn't going to hurt me. I wasn't going to die. I learned that however overwhelming an obstacle looks, you just have to take the first step—like going up the pole, where I didn't even think about the height, I thought about the journey to the top."

The philosophy behind this workshop was that even the smallest adventures could translate to the rest of a daring golfer's life. As Steve Cohen, the true architect behind the weekend, said, "In every round of golf, as in every day of our lives, issues of self-confidence, awareness, fear, and trust present themselves. How do we react? And how willing are we to risk new ways of reacting?" He suggested that the lessons gained this weekend would provide a source of reflection for how we live. Or to put it another way, the workshop was a sort of practice tee for confronting fear and contemplating adventure in our lives. Cohen said, "Golf is a perfect metaphor for the exploration of personal transformation and growth."

And in fact, several weeks after our stint in Kohler, John Shaffer reported that something inside of him had been transformed. One of his usual golf partners noticed it right away, commenting that Shaffer suddenly displayed a quiet confidence. His golf scores also improved dramatically.

And another thing. Since returning home, Shaffer had become more aggressively confident in business. He said, "There have been three people I've wanted to talk to forever, but I thought there wasn't a chance of getting them as clients. The workshop gave me an inner sense of worth and I wasn't afraid to present for their business, even though the odds were infinitesimal that I'll get it. Maybe that goes hand in hand with my ropes course experience."

Even Steve Heller, whose own adventure had been dealing with the fear of choosing not to take on the ropes course, and of choosing to play from the white tees, came away with something valuable. Heller reflected that being able to express himself and his desires clearly in the workshop allowed him to consider taking more risks regarding his feelings at home. Referring to a more emotional type of adventure, Heller reported, "Anything that helps me share how I feel is worthwhile."

Did my own life change as a result of Golfing on the Edge? From a purely golf-centric perspective, I would have to say: well, maybe. Soon after the workshop my handicap dropped to 11.9, its lowest number by far in the twenty-five years I've been playing the game. Whether jumping off perfectly good telephone poles and holding hands with other scared golfers was responsible, I can't answer definitively. And is that even the point? Not exactly, according to Steve Cohen, who relishes offering this toast at Shivas Irons Society events: "Beware the quicksands of perfection. Fuck our ever getting better."

As for the rest of my life, in the months following the workshop I started several new, risky creative ventures, and made a seemingly bold and dangerous move in my personal life that I will not elaborate upon here. I also undertook some spontaneous third-world travel—something I'd not done in a decade. I understand that how these events turned out is beside the point; the important thing was that I managed to take on these challenges at all. Like John Shaffer and even Steve Heller and maybe other workshop participants, I learned to deal with my fear and—in several different ways—to jump. Coincidence or cause and effect? Does it really matter?

The greatest adventures explore the rugged and uneven and sometimes fescue-lined wilderness of the territory within, and that, of course, is the point. The added advantage of a golf adventure is that you can also pick up a hot dog and a Snickers bar at the turn.

PART TWO

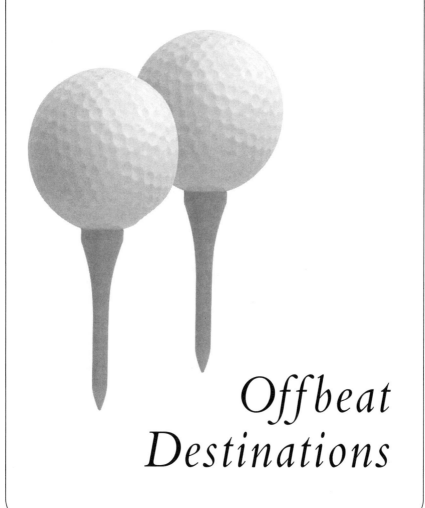

Offbeat Destinations

5

Fear and Loathing
(mostly fear)
in St. Andrews

THE MORNING WAS cold and a cutting wind blew over the Old Course like a knee in the groin. As my friend and fellow golf writer Tom Harack and I watched a couple of guys we knew teeing off on the first hole of the most famous golf layout on the planet—a gorgeous, rugged place of power and pilgrimage, a sacred place of homecoming and deep emotion—we huddled close in the freshening breeze and whispered "Miss it. *Miss it!*" at their backswings.

Despite the weather, a ragged gallery clustered around the first tee: golfers awaiting their times, caddies milling about smoking, townsfolk shuffling off to work, and endless brigades of tourists circling the Royal and Ancient Clubhouse in goofy wonder, toting shopping bags full of logoed sweaters and drink coasters, clubhead covers, T-shirts, tartan neckties, boxer shorts, jockstraps, condoms, hollow-point bullets, and Lord only knew what else, all sporting the famous St. Andrews crest. They stood in awe, these spectators, with quiet smiles on their lips and envy blossoming in their hearts, all of them, I think it is safe to say, repeating—consciously or not—the same mantra: "Miss it. *Miss it!*"

I began developing this bitter and cynical attitude toward St. Andrews several years ago when I visited Scotland to gather material for my first book. My friend Tom Liszewski, who runs an excellent golf travel service called Golf Vacations, in Boston, was kind enough to set up my itinerary. Although Tom managed to book complimentary tee times on eleven great golf courses throughout Scotland (many of which he arranged for me to play with club secretaries or other dignitaries), and although he scored free hotel rooms (including a suite at the Balmoral in Edinburgh that was so large I got lost looking for the bathroom late one night), Tom was unable to secure anything from the Royal and Ancient besides a snooty letter.

The circumstances surrounding this current visit did little to improve my attitude. Despite the fact that I'd traveled more than six thousand miles, on three airplanes, in coach, and then climbed aboard a bus for a three-hour ride to spend a mere four days in St. Andrews; regardless that I was a guest of the posh Old Course Hotel, which practically straddles the famous Road Hole; and without consideration that our group of golf writers had been invited here specifically to write about and promote golf in St. Andrews, the reigning powers wouldn't even guarantee us a tee time on the Old Course. St. Andrews also threw bunker sand in our faces by insisting that we'd have to pay the hundred-dollar green fees—if they even deemed us worthy to jab our spikes in their grass.

Throughout my life I have always felt as though I am somehow special, and that rules don't apply to me. My mother confronted me with this fact several million times during my childhood, and though it pains me to say so, my mother was right. So when the Royal and Ancient royally kicked me in my egotism for the second time I grew angry and vengeful. But behind these easy emotions, of course, cowered fear and helplessness over a situation in which something I so badly wanted lay beyond my own control—an experience that most avid golfers can probably relate to.

After our companions hit successful tee shots on the first hole of the Old Course and chased happily after them, and still half an hour before Tom's and my own tee time, I asked the starter if there wasn't someplace we could retreat indoors to get warm while we waited. From inside his toasty booth he raised a steaming mug of tea in mock "cheers," threw his head back, and laughed like one of us was insane.

(Okay; he actually told me I could walk half a block to the Woolen Mills Store, but I distinctly noticed that he said this with an *attitude*—though maybe that was just his accent.)

Scotsmen have been playing golf on the location of the Old Course in St. Andrews for more than five hundred years. In 1552 a local archbishop passed a decree granting the townspeople the right to pursue "gaof, futeball, and shuting" on the local links in perpetuity. Although the archbishop wasn't much of a speller, his word was law. Approximately 60 percent of the available tee times on the Old Course are currently reserved for town residents, who still play there as if it were a semiprivate club. Which in fact it is.

But chances are that you're not a Scotsman. So if you'd like to play golf on the most famous course in the noosphere, good luck. And get in line. If you didn't happen to book a tee time a year in advance, the only way to secure this rare commodity is to enter the daily ballot. Every afternoon, the powers of the Royal and Ancient randomly select lucky balloteers to fill open tee times for the following day. While the chances are good that you'll get on if you're in town for a while, it is also entirely possible that you won't. Although I'd been working hard not to measure myself by such external circumstances, I couldn't help feeling that my success or failure in the ballot would provide a physical manifestation of my accrued golf karma: Only a loser would travel so far to come here and not even get on the course. Detachment was not an easy lesson to master.

Learning that we had to enter the ballot fattened me with further anger and disdain, and elicited that spoiled-brat head shaking that my mother tried so tirelessly to cure me of. But I have since come to realize that while the ballot system is as arbitrary as sacrificing a virgin to the volcano gods, it is perfectly philosophical for the same reason: It allows Providence to decide whether we are, in fact, worthy of playing golf on the game's most sacred layout. And that is the pure and unarguable beauty of the system: that it remains—just as our best golf rounds most often do—beyond willful control. I had no choice but to throw a tantrum or let go—and I wasn't entirely sure which constituted a better course of action.

On our first afternoon in St. Andrews, Tom Harack and another golf writer and I played a joyful, disorientedly jet-lagged round of golf on the town's Jubilee Course, finishing just as the stone-gray buildings and the blue sea sopped up the last pools of afternoon light. Upon sinking my final putt I skipped back to my room in anticipation only to discover that we had not, in fact, been awarded a tee time on the Old Course for the next day.

So instead, we made our way 'round the excellent Duke's Course, an inland layout designed by five-time Open champion Peter Thomson, and owned by our friends at the Old Course Hotel. Tom and I competed against two staffers from *Senior Golfer Magazine* in a two-dollar Nassau. The course itself pitched and rolled and undulated musically among pines and birches, through varicolored grasses, over burns, around ponds, and past patches of heather and gorse, but all I could focus on was our stupid, stupid bet. Though I'd been hoping to shoot in the low eighties in preparation for breaking through to a new personal best on the Old Course should I merit the opportunity to play there, I would have needed to cheat just to break a hundred that day on the Duke's. And I seemed perpetually married to performance.

After lunch in the stately clubhouse, Tom (having earned the new nickname Bunker Boy) and I caught a ride to the Ladybank Golf Club—an Open qualifying site—to see if we couldn't rescue the respectable remnants of our games. While this morning's sorry impetus was to win a two-dollar Nassau, this afternoon presented me with an even more senseless goal. Although only five of us were playing golf on this press trip, our hosts had promised to award prizes for the lowest score on each course each day, the lowest overall score, and the best Stableford tally. This afternoon, since Tom was the only other golfer (and since his putting stroke seems like a desperate cry for help), I figured my chances were pretty good to turn in the low net. And oh, what an admirable role model I'd be!

I recognized the small, small pitiful nature of my desire to "win," yet I still proved incapable of letting go of performance. I played ignominiously and with great self-consciousness, barely noticing the elegant pines, the way the steep bunkers cast rounded shadows, the pewter, cerulean, and orange colors of the sky. At dusk we crawled home to learn once again that we had not been granted the honor of playing the Old Course the next day.

That night I tussled with a kicky eighteen-year-old Scotch at the Road Hole Bar in our hotel. Then I ate far too much good food, drank too much Merlot, and excused myself at eleven. But I was too restless to sleep, so at midnight I pulled on some clothes and went walking.

I ambled out behind the hotel along a shell path that ran beside the seventeenth hole (the Road Hole) of the Old Course. After glancing feloniously to make sure no one else was about, I crossed onto the most well-known fairway in golf, feeling an illicit thrill. I sneaked between the deep bunkers and up to the green.

Standing next to the pin, with a light rain tinkling and the world dark around me, I felt a weird cocktail of fear and longing and a schoolboy sort of love for the place I was standing. And all at once my anger broke up and drained away. I am not embarrassed to admit that I whispered a quiet prayer. I prayed not for a tee time, or to break eighty, to meet a mermaid, or for my books to sell a million copies. I prayed for the courage to be able to play golf—and to live—without fear.

My anger, I recognized right then, as the night wind blew over the linkslands, was a cheap suit dressing up the fear of not getting what I wanted. I was mad at the R&A because they had failed to recognize me as someone special. As I appealed to whatever spirits ruled this place it came clear to me that I live my life afraid of almost everything: of not performing well, or of what other folks might think of me; of slicing a tee shot or blading a pitch or three-putting a green; of letting go of control enough to let someone get intimate; of wearing the wrong shoes or choosing the incorrect fork or spilling red wine on my white shirt. And, mostly, of making bad choices and being treated unfairly and not getting what's coming to me. Yet instead of acknowledging my fears, I disguise them with anger, often fooling even myself about how I really feel. This has been the self-protective and deceitful architecture of my life, and the very thing that Fred Shoemaker, Ed LeBeau, Chuck Hogan, and Steve Cohen had tried to help me deconstruct so that I might live more fully and—incidentally—play better golf.

Standing beside the wind-rippled flag of the Road Hole as rain percussed around me and clouds obscured the moon, I even feared catching cold or ruining my coat. I tried to let go. I breathed deeply into my solar plexus. I pledged to live differently and more fully. I asked for help, and to be worthy of the honor of playing golf here. I let the rain fall without wishing it would stop, knowing that the rain couldn't give a rip about what I wished or knew.

Eventually I stepped toward the eighteenth green, crossed Swilcan Bridge, circled the Royal and Ancient clubhouse, and continued down to where the burn tongued into the North Sea. Looking out over the water I thought about my life and how it had

led me here. Some students from the university waltzed drunken-
ly past and I grew skittish, afraid they might speak to me and interrupt my solitude. I tightened, then laughed at yet another example
of my fear.

After listening to the breakers playing a beat of *whoosh-whoosh-
boom* against the shore, I retraced my steps toward the hotel. Walking
across the shared first/eighteenth fairway, I felt the soft turf relenting
under my shoes. And then, looking up, I spotted a pair of headlights
advancing toward me down the path adjacent to the hole. From atop
the vehicle a searchlight swept back and forth over the links, comb-
ing the grassy expanse with light.

The car was still two hundred yards away, and as it crept steadily
closer I knew I had enough time to sprint for cover, to throw myself
down in a bunker or press my body flat against one of the rolling
mounds that made for such difficult lies. But I also recognized that I
was being tested. I understood that the challenges of this golf course
were not limited to hitting a ball with a stick.

As the vehicle closed the gap between us, everything in me
shouted, *Flee! run! hide! get out of the way before you're exposed!* But
another voice—calm, unfamiliar, slightly officiously superherolike—
reminded me there was nothing to be afraid of.

Run, moron! the first voice hollered.

I sank my hands into the pockets of my field coat, squinched my
eyes at the darkness, and strode ahead. I kept walking, though fear
and adrenaline protested my aplomb. Just before the searchlight illu-
minated my terror and horns blared and security sprinted across the
sacred grass to tackle me and drag me away, the light simply went
out. The vehicle drove close, closer, parallel, and then past me. And
then the light went back on. I strolled back to my hotel, laughing,
and slept hard.

The next morning, my Scottish friend and former college soc-
cer coach John Wallace, whom I hadn't seen in fourteen years, drove

down to St. Andrews from his home in nearby Fraserburgh for a day
of golf. He and Tom and I rode over to Crail and played the gorgeous links course there in wind and sun and hail and cool rain,
smoking good cigars, telling old stories and inventing some new
ones. On the first tee I relinquished the scorecard to Tom and
stopped chafing about numbers—even when I hit into a deep
bunker on the ninth and flailed on several shots before escaping.
Even after slicing my drive into the ocean on an easy par five. Even
after three-putting a flat green. I simply valued the camaraderie, the
chance to play this beautiful game with friends who lived far away,
and whom I might not see again anytime soon. I just played. Played!
Like a boy. I shot eighty-nine, Tom informed me, as we sped home
for a quick lunch before venturing out on St. Andrews' New Course
in the afternoon. The voices of my many coaches were lost in the
simple purity of surf crashing on the beach.

    We teed off at just after three o'clock and the starter warned us
we wouldn't have time to finish, but we agreed among ourselves to
canter briskly between shots. Somehow hurrying from lie to lie
improved our games. I sank several long, unconscious putts. We all
hit the green on a 225-yard blind par three into the wind. We golfed
back toward town beneath an engaging drama of clouds and light,
rainbows and salty air. We finished chilled and windburned and
happy as could be, all lipping out cross-country putts on the eighteenth green as the sky darkened above us. We veered directly to the
Jigger Inn for two rounds of Lagavulin's peaty single malt chased by
Scottish ale. The day had delivered everything that golf could
promise: heroics and tragedy, good friends, moody weather, laughter
and connection, and a sense of tramping proudly on and belonging
to this great, great earth. I shot eighty-five, Tom told me after adding
up our scores in the bar.

    Entering the warm haven of my room at the Old Course Hotel
with an equally warm buzz, I anticipated nothing. I suddenly possessed everything a man could desire.

But a message awaited me: "Congratulations," it read. "Your tee time on the Old Course is reserved for 10:30 tomorrow."

On the first tee of the Old Course I torqued and stretched and tried to loosen up in the clenching wind. I teed up a spanking-new Titleist and considered the widest fairway in golf. I acknowledged again that I had lived much of my life out of fear, and I prayed for the grace to play this round of golf free from such worry. I stuffed my notebook in my bag, understanding that it was far more important to live in the moment and really experience playing this golf course than it was to ponder what I might write about the experience later on. I have hidden behind my notebook for nearly twenty years, safely insulated from my own life by intellectual abstraction. Today I vowed to pull that curtain aside.

I launched a beautiful tee shot high into the prevailing wind and watched it sail above the fairway. Then I hit a lofted wedge over Swilcan Burn and onto the back edge of the huge green. From that distance I was content with a three putt for bogey.

I don't remember much of the next seven holes; they were pure beyond description, and to talk about them somehow takes something away.

I would like to tell you that my life changed on the Old Course that day, that I subdued a demon that had ridden piggyback on my consciousness, strangling spontaneity since I was a boy.

I will tell you this: Standing on the eighth green after snaking in a long putt to save par, I realized that I was two over, and something opened up in me like a sky suddenly pouring rain, and I started to cry. Cry! I couldn't stand still. My hands numbed with cold, and as I went and peed in the gorse while we waited for the group ahead of us to move out of range on the ninth hole, I recognized that I was having a career round, that I'd parred six out of the first eight holes and nearly parred the other two. Chilly tears broke sharply over the upper tier of my cheekbones. I cried—with joy for what had just happened, with fear, and with detachment from fear, all the while realizing that I would not get what I wanted. Not yet. Not today. I let go in a way that I cannot explain, accepting something that on this day ruined my excellent chance to break eighty because it was too precious to hold on to. I celebrated the magic of St. Andrews with a good cry and tossed anger and control into the October wind like blades of grass.

On the ninth tee I knew I was about to chunk my drive fifty yards ahead into the heather. But I swung hard anyway, without fear or attachment. The ball flew exactly where I'd expected. My heart sailed off in the air currents, floating high and then dropping like a stone.

My caddie advised me to execute a practice swing in the heather to feel how it would grab my club. I did so, thinking: *So what if I miss? This is golf. A game. Enjoy the challenge. Let go. Be free.*

It was the one of the last such pure and joyous shots I hit that day. But I didn't fucking care.

6

Oregon Road Trip:
The Bender Through Bend

IMAGINE A ROAD trip where two men motor six hundred miles (crossing two mountain ranges and dozens of rivers) in one long weekend to play ninety holes of golf at four resorts, misplace seven sleeves of balls, smoke eight cigars, mountain bike miles of single-track, slug three gallons of coffee, draw eleven blackjacks, quaff innumerable local microbrews, and chat up two cart girls and a handful of future LPGA pros. Here's how it's done.

DAY 1

My buddy John Hayden and I wake in the middle of the night (okay, actually it's six-thirty) and we're on the road in his VW Westphalia camper by six-fifty, triple espressos in hand. A woman could never get ready this fast, although she might offer certain other advantages over John. Our destination: the Resort at the Mountain, in Welches, an hour east of my home in Portland. This Scottish-themed playground features three old-style mountain golf nines—Pine Cone, Thistle, and Foxglove—that climb and dip like the recent NASDAQ market, samba along creeks and rivers, and tiptoe euphorically among old-growth fir and cedar. The small greens and rolling fairways lend a Donald Rossian feel, but recent renovations by architect John Harbottle, and loving and environmentally enhancing improvements by owner Ed Hopper, have brought this stately lay-out into the modern era. The longest eighteen plays to roughly 6,500 yards of pristine alpine golf. John and I wish we could stay longer at this cozy mountain retreat, but the highway calls. Loudly. Crankily.

As the Westy wheezes over Mount Hood we consider stopping for a couple of bomber ski runs on the Palmer Glacier, but we need to make some miles. An hour later we're cruising through redrock canyons on the Warm Springs Indian Reservation, home to Kahneeta Resort and our "back eighteen" of the day. Kahneeta's short, perky layout routes beneath the dusty buttes, red cliffs, and rugged western topography of Oregon's high desert east of the Cascades. It's a low-scoring course with five par threes and five par fives (two are reachable at 486 and 488 yards) and wide fairways buffered by scruffy trees. Head pro Joe Rauschenburg joins us on the second nine, which John and I mostly spend looking for chunked drives and wondering if we'll finish before dark. Oh yes—and also wondering how we've gotten to suck so bad since this morning.

"Want a tip from the pro?" Joe asks, after I shank another Titleist into the native grass.

I nod, expecting a swing correction that might resurrect me from golfing Hades.

"Play earlier," he says, laughing.

That night, John and I have a few laughs of our own as we clean out the Indian casino of nearly ten bucks—each!—playing blackjack and schmoozing the princess who's dealing. When cigarette smoke threatens to obscure our view of the cards, we head for our lodging: an actual tepee beside Kahneeta's hot springs pool. We fall asleep try-ing to puzzle out the possible golfological relationship between *tepee* and *TPC*.

DAY 2

No time to linger after an early dip in the hot pool. We saved enough money sleeping in a tepee, for godsakes, to splurge on the Crosswater package at Sunriver Resort just south of Bend. The package includes a woodsy suite with fireplace and entrée onto one of the best golf courses in the noosphere. Crosswater is aptly named, as it plays over rivers, wetlands, ponds, and puddles of tears cried by golfers overwhelmed by the views of snowcapped volcanic peaks. The John Fought/Bob Cupp design is as beautiful and punishing as a supermodel, but John and I are up to the challenge from the 6,185-yard white tees with the help of several locally brewed adult beverages and a couple of stubby Upmanns. To give you an idea of the potential carnage, Crosswater's twelfth hole plays a mere 572 yards from the whites—it's 687 from the tips—and features a lake (or is that an entire ocean?) from tee to nasty green. Still, we rule!

And then we nap. Hard. Then rally into biking clothes for a rollicking ride on the Deschutes River Trail, a dipsy single-track that slaloms between ponderosa pines and roams between lava fields and open meadows beside crashing waterfalls. En route, we abandon our plan to turn around halfway; although it's nearly dark and we have no air pump, we pedal all the way into the sportropolis of Bend—having no idea of the distance—and stop at Honkers, the first bar we see. We glug Full Sail Ambers and I tell John about the nearby Deschutes Brewery, a bar full of Lycra-clad bikers, chalky climbers, heavy-breathing kayakers, and other hottie sport girls. But we opt instead for a cab to haul our sorry asses and dusty bikes back to Sunriver, and settle for a nightcap at the Owl's Nest bar. An excellent choice, it turns out, because the NCAA women's golf championship starts at Sunriver tomorrow, and some of the players are working on their short games by drinking Cosmopolitans.

DAY 3

I won't talk about last night except to say please don't tell the Purdue team John's real name. We wake at five-thirty, slam a pot of coffee, and stumble around Sunriver's hangover-friendly Meadows Course, which is as welcoming as a panting retriever, and—at first light—emptier than a Chicago Bulls game. Directional bunkers aid our wobbly setups, and the greens of this 7,012-yard track are big enough to see with one eye closed. After breakfasting on eighteen delicious holes set in meadows and pines by John Fought, we're fortified for the five-hour drive over Santiam Pass, across the winery-rich Willamette Valley, through the Coast Range, and finally to the Pacific. We skip naptime today and head right for the windswept Salishan Golf Links, a whiskey-rough 6,439-yard affair in Gleneden Beach. The frisky front side rambles through forests that echo the sounds of mis-hit three-woods. The delightfully playful back scampers along dunes and beach grasses in a bracing salt breeze. As usual, we finish golfing in the dark.

That night Salishan Lodge (once rated as the only five-star motel in America) is full and our wallets are nearly empty anyway, so we opt for a supermarket dinner (read: half a rack of Black Butte Porter, jerky, salsa, and chips) and free lodging at the Westphalia Inn—John's camper. We're surprised to learn that you can find a perfect crash spot even in a state park that prohibits camping. We fall asleep in our golf shoes while discussing where to go out to that night.

7

Golfing Gourmet:
Hawaii Bites

I'M STANDING ON the tee box of the world-renowned third hole of the Mauna Kea Golf Course on the Big Island of Hawaii with a lot on my mind. If this two-hundred-yard par three that plays almost exclusively over blue surf crashing on black lava were any more famous it would be sleeping with Madonna. If it were any more daunting I might have a wetting accident. Yet I'm not fretting over club selection or wind or even my alignment: I'm obsessing about a chef.

Well, a dozen of them, actually: For example, Hapuna Beach Prince Hotel's executive chef Corey Waite, whom—while a pretty good golfer himself despite his hockey slapshot of a swing—is more impressive with a saucepan than a six-iron. As I tee my ball up on the sharp edge of this volcanic island, two windy football fields from a cup smaller than a soup tureen (and unfortunately not filled with seafood bisque), I visualize Corey's Pesto Lobster Tail with Truffle Spring Roll and Kahua Spinach Salad, practically feeling the tender and crunchy textures all the way to my toes. As I take an obligatory practice swing, I see myself lifting my fork before daintily biting into a Seared Breast of Duck with Sweet Potato Mash in Black Cherry Zinfandel Sauce, created by personable Maui Prince Hotel executive chef Greg Gaspar. If I'm going to finish playing this famous golf course without collapsing into a puddle of drool, I'd better stop thinking about the other seven courses that await me at dinner tonight.

You, too, can face a long weekend full of such challenges as playing some superlative oceanside golf, cavorting in the warm Pacific, bedding down at a couple of fine hotels, and being fed by a dozen men and women who could drive Julia Child into a high-pitched, cleaver-wielding jealous rage. Just attend Mauna Kea Resort's Winter Wine Escape, for heaven's sake. And put down that filleting knife!

Nearly a decade old, this great Escape draws chefs from some of America's best restaurants and fixes them up with a barrel of top-shelf vintners for a three-day festival of gastronomy that's not unlike astronomy—star-studded, and with food that's out of this world. Choose from nine events—including the seven-course Concerto of Food and Wine, and the California Classics wine tasting—held over three days at the neighboring and stellar Mauna Kea Beach and Hapuna Beach Prince Hotels.

On opening night, I attended the Prelude in the airy Hapuna courtyard. The Azure McCall Band was barely audible over the sounds of chewing and dreamy sighs. Attendees, who floated happily between food booths, were unusually friendly and talkative. Participating chefs and vintners were welcoming and willing to educate. Eminently lovable Shawn McClain (TRIOS Restaurant, Chicago) lured folks to his table with an artistic Grilled Sea Bass, Napa Cabbage, Smoked Bacon, Manila Clams, and Endamame Truffled Corn Chowder that married land and sea in perfect harmony. I didn't even know what *endamame* meant, but I ran to him like a puppy. A moment later I fell hard for a Grilled Pork Tenderloin with Smoked Jasmine Rice, Mustard Greens, and Kiawe Honey Gastrique conjured by magician-chef Michael Otsuka (Verbena-Gramercy Park Restaurant, New York). The sweet and smoky flavors made the meat sing like Bob Marley.

Between bites, I talked with vintners such as Brian Talley, who poured smooth samples of his diligent work. After investigating more dishes than my spandex belt could accommodate, I concluded my evening on the breezeway overlooking Kauna'oa Beach and the stars of other galaxies, which I'm guessing couldn't even cook up a decent Daikon Ponzu. My waistline and I prepared to leave, but were enticed back by Paul Mugnier of Premium Ports and Madeiras, who forced us to taste several dessert wines to accompany our lonely La Perla Habana. Finally, I made a break for the shuttle back to Mauna Kea because, as one guest warned me, you should never drink and drive: You might spill your drink.

The next morning I woke well before noon to play the Hapuna Golf Course with head professional Ron Castillo, who applauded my accomplishment of using up two containers of divot mix, and did not report me to the superintendent. Castillo is the steward of a challenging 6,875-yard Arnold Palmer design that—much like a well-cooked lobster—requires some work to savor its varied delights. The mountainish target course calls for laser tee shots across ample hazards, and offers ocean views from every last hole. Castillo, who inherited a familywide golf gene (rumor has it that his sister kicks the most Castillo), informed me that all of the par fives were reachable in two if I was willing to assume certain risks. He added that past performance was no guarantee of future results.

But despite the many charms of the golf course, the round was just a ruse to pass the time before my next meal. That evening I attended the premier Concerto event in Mauna Kea's Batik Restaurant. Following an open-air champagne reception, we retired to a table sparkling with crates of flatware and enough wineglasses to make me wonder if the Waterfords themselves might be joining us.

The seven-course orgy of deliciousness included a daringly simple Quick Sauté of Zucchini, Toasted Almonds, and Pecorino prepared by chef Jimmy Bradley (Red Cat Restaurant, New York), who was spotted cooking himself on the beach that afternoon. Bradley's zucchini was paired with a 1995 Far Niente Chardonnay that smartly framed the light crispness of the vegetables. Chef Thomas Woods, of Mauna Kea Beach Hotel, presented the evening's strongest dish—

moist Noisettes of Veal Marchand de Vin with a sweetly energetic Tomato Onion Marmalade. Woods's veal was tag-teamed with a wine that my dinner partner, a full-time food writer, described as "tasting of smoked ham." While a couple of the wine pairings struck us as unusual, the overall effect of the dinner was stunning. Which is to say we were all a bit stunned as we retired outside to sip Graham's 20-Year Tawny Port and puff on the intriguing, nutty, short-but-handsome Don Lino Havana Reserves.

I believe it was a vintage 1996 Top Flite XL that I sailed into the woods on the fourth hole of the Mauna Kea Golf Course the next morning, in the company of professional Brad Baptist, whose greatest challenge was to repair my rather extraordinary form. Mauna Kea, designed by Robert Trent Jones in the 1960s, has long been one of the classic venues of Hawaiian golf (burp!). In addition to the so-famous-it-wears-sunglasses third hole, there are actually seventeen others, carved out of black lava and largely characterized by fairways as wide and welcoming as a cedar-planked salmon, florets of broccoliesque rough, and layer-cakian elevation changes (oh, pardon me!).

Finally done with some of the most highly regarded oceanside golf (be . . . l ch) known to man, I capped off my weekend of digestible debauchery at the Finale, held on Mauna Kea's south lawn, overlooking the ocean. While the Lim Family performed traditional Hawaiian dances, I followed my own family tradition of consuming enormous amounts of food. Each guest chef gripped and ripped his Calphalon to serve up two final offerings.

Jimmy Bradley's adorably juicy Mini Venison Burgers, and chef David Robins's (Spago Restaurant, Las Vegas) Shrimp and Calamari Ceviche—like a sea-breezy sailboat ride—won the evening for me. That is, until I reached the front of the long dessert line. As a highly trained professional guest, I felt obligated to try the Coconut Mousse; Apple Fritters and Cinnamon Ice Cream; Pineapple Cream with Blue Hawaiian Coconut Sauce; and the richly intriguing Deep Chocolate Cake. Somebody had to. And you weren't there.

8

Before the Fall:
Golfing Baja California

ONCE THERE WAS a place where, as blazing desert temperatures cooled in late afternoon and the sun staggered toward a tropical ocean, your toughest decision might have been choosing among a handful of world-class golf courses designed by Jack Nicklaus, Robert Trent Jones Jr., or the Dye Corporation; where you could drive to the clubhouse listening to salsa music on the radio, and an assistant pro would rush out to grab your golf bag and strap it to a cart, fill your cooler with bottled water and soft drinks and icy Tecate beer, and send you off—*vaya con dios*—to play in quiet so intense you'd hear lizards blinking in the shade of giant cardon cacti. Where you might not glimpse another human until the turn, when the pro met you with a fresh cooler. Where, in the shimmering distance, the Sea of Cortez sparkled blue beyond the mesquite trees. If these recollections sound better to you than what you're doing now, grab your sunscreen and head on down to Mexico's Baja California. But hurry. Because at this very moment construction crews are toiling 'round the clock to erect tens of thousands of homes and condos and hotel rooms; public relations firms are cranking out press releases; and someday soon things will all be changed.

Until recently, Baja—a strip of mountainous desert that broke off from the Mexican mainland along the San Andreas Fault a couple of million years ago, and which now pokes its skinny finger between the Pacific Ocean and the Sea of Cortez—was populated by local lobstermen, international sport fishermen, wrecked cars, and a few American retirees in Winnebagos who spoke the sort of mock Spanish sure to enrage the natives. A few decades ago, the peninsula was discovered by sea kayakers, whale-watchers, and bicyclists inspired by its rugged remoteness.

But more recently, Fonatur—an arm of the Mexican government created to develop mega-resort destinations and attract private investment—set out to reinvent Baja as the new Mexican Riviera. So if you'd like to be one of those old codgers who can reminisce about a special place before developers ruined it, make a run for the border. Pronto. Once construction is finished, tourists will likely follow like sailfish striking bait. And if Fonatur succeeds here like they did in Cancún and Ixtapa, Baja is doomed. Which is to say it will mutate into an excellent, overbuilt golf destination combining the attractions, high prices, and crowds of Phoenix, Maui, and Palm Springs. Except the golf will be even better.

The remotest of Baja's top golf properties is located in Loreto, halfway between the U.S. border and Los Cabos—the tip of the peninsula where most of the real estate feeding frenzy is taking place. The Mexican public relations machine describes Loreto as "where, even the mountains swim"—whatever that means. The Spanish built Baja's first mission here nearly three hundred years ago, but the real invasion has barely begun.

Although the Inn at Loreto (formerly the Stouffer Presidente) is a perfectly fine hotel, its four-star rating may mislead if you expect such numbers to correspond to American resort ratings. Outside, the inn sports lovely island decor, a tranquil swimming bay, and soothing palm-shaded courtyards. Inside, guest rooms are merely adequate. But Campo de Golf Loreto makes even press release descriptions sound almost understated. Designed by Pedro Guereca and Mario Schjetan Danton, the course is as full of great surprises as its architects are unknown in the United States.

I played Loreto with charming caddie master Jose Villareal, who possessed an interesting job title since the course didn't actually have any caddies. Villareal learned golf only two years previous, yet was really the head pro. And the assistant pro. He also managed the driving range until, as he explained to me, "somebody stole the ball." Loreto begins like an Arizona desert course, with islands of cushy Tidwarf floating in vast expanses of sharp, scrubby flora. Unlike Arizona, the layout leaps across ocean inlets and meanders down to a rocky shore and—in the distance— the red La Giganta Mountains pyramid upward into the denim-blue sky. You'll do well to ask about the Spanish word for "mercy" when playing great holes like the fourteenth, a 220-yard par three that begins from a cliff-hugging tee box and plays across a lagoon and a wedge of sandy beach. My compadre's watch alarm went off during my backswing here, but my second three-wood cleared the hazards and I allowed myself to think I'd made a legitimate par. To help me on the green, Villareal advised that all putts break toward the ocean, but he didn't say which one.

From Loreto, head for Los Cabos, which consists of the towns of Cabo San Lucas and San Jose del Cabo (much quieter). Split the middle by proceeding directly to the Palmilla Hotel, between the two, and only leave the hallowed grounds to play golf.

You'll come upon this very special hideaway at the end of a road lined with stately palms. The whitewashed adobe buildings sport graceful arches and red tile roofs. Fountains plash in stone patios, and jasmine and gardenias cast sweet-scented shade. My Vista suite featured plantation shutters, ceiling fan, and a tiled bathroom large enough to practice corner kicks for the World Cup. My own patio provided the perfect place to breakfast on fresh rolls and coffee while being hypnotized by crashing surf below.

Built in the 1950s by the son of former Mexican president Abelando Rodriguez, the Palmilla was once accessible only by boat or private plane. It still had no phones or TVs in the rooms. John Wayne and Bing Crosby stayed here on fishing trips (not together); more recent guests include Goldie Hawn, Dustin Hoffman, and Joe Montana. The hotel earned Mexico's highest rating—Gran Turismo Clase Especial—and is worthy of every last bit of hype.

So, too, is the resort's Jack Nicklaus golf course. The Mountain and Arroyo nines recall Jack's design at Tucson's La Paloma, but they also demonstrate how much he's learned since then. The course incorporates ocean, desert, and mountains into a dramatic track with an unbelievable fright quotient and tons of daunting carries from the 7,100-yard, 144-sloped back tees. But from the other four sets of tees the course isn't simply shorter; it's four completely different courses. At its easiest it plays forty-nine hundred yards with a 109 slope— providing for an incredible range of golf experiences. Even at its most intimidating, it's still fair and playable.

The course offers so many great holes that can play so many ways, you'll grow weary figuring all the permutations. And every hole offers views of the Sea of Cortez and Sierra Laguna Mountains. Many of the bright green fairways are defined by golden arroyos. Deep, wide chasms dare you to be a hero, but may leave you bleating like a sheep. Number six on the Mountain side begins with what looks like a gigundo carry, but a great drive may actually carry through the fairway. Your second shot recrosses the same arroyo and must drop onto a lovely, welcoming bowl-shaped green. The Arroyo nine at Palmilla is shorter and easier, and the Ocean side provides a couple of dramatic seaside holes. While he was already in Mexico, Jack also found time to design the nearby Cabo Del Sol golf course, which various press releases quote him as calling "the most magnificent" or simply "the best" piece of property he's ever seen. In spite of the obvious fluffery, it's tough to argue as you struggle to catch your breath on no less than seven oceanside holes. This natural, rugged, windy course recalls Scotland in spite of desert, mountains, and hot, dry air—perhaps because so little earth was moved in constructing it, and because the layout rests so comfortably within the landscape. Five sets of tees stretch the track from 4,696 to 7,037 yards.

In a breach of modesty, Jack has also been quoted as saying of Cabo Del Sol, "I firmly believe that these are the three best finishing holes in all of golf." Or the two best, depending on which press release you read. Still, he may be right. Many players are comparing this course to Pebble Beach (of course, I've yet to play a new layout that players didn't compare to Pebble Beach). The signature seventeenth plays 173 yards from the back over crashing waves, rocky outcroppings, sandy beach, rotting shipwrecks, killer whales, sea monsters, and alien pod farms. The finishing hole, at 425 yards, hugs the contours of the shoreline and doglegs to a large seaside green. Other highlights include back-to-back oceanside par threes on the front nine. I was lucky enough to play Cabo Del Sol before four hotels and thirty-four hundred residences undermined Jack's work the way a fig leaf ruins a classical Greek statue.

But lest Jack Nicklaus have a monopoly on golf in Los Cabos, the Cabo Real resort offers sturdy competition. Although they originally hired Joe Finger to design their golf holes, when management learned that Nicklaus was setting up shop down the road, they sought more clout and handed the project over to Robert Trent Jones Jr., who drew up thirty-six holes.

Jones created a tough, muscular design on a comparatively second-rate piece of property. At times, Cabo Real's holes seem crowded, and pass too close to the road—but maybe anyplace would look bad after seeing Nicklaus's local efforts. In fact, Jones's signature free-form bunkers and small, elevated greens, combined with fairways that play along ridgetops and offer expansive views, make for a fabulous track. The first six holes here climb steadily; subsequent holes descend to a few oceanside challenges before winding back up to the clubhouse. Five sets of tees stretching from 5,198 to 7,058 yards, and sloped from 114 to 141, offer plenty of fun for the whole family. And speaking of fun, one woman told me that while raking one of the oversoft bunkers after playing out of it, she found three other balls buried in the trap.

Not to be outdone, either, in sheer magnitude of development, Cabo Real was designed to feature seven hotels, fifteen hundred condos, and 450 homes. The Melia Cabo Real offers a lively large-scale hotel experience with a huge glass pyramid floating above the lobby, much rattan scattered about, a pool complex including water volleyball and swim-up bar, and such toys as WaveRunners, paddle bikes, and sea kayaks available on the wide beach below the hotel.

And if Los Cabos didn't already offer enough great new golf— and it does, it does—the Dye Corporation (Pete, his late brother Roy, and Roy's son, Matt) built the Cabo San Lucas Country Club, which was mostly designed to sell eighteen hundred homesites. The flattish course features typically sharp Dye edges, straight-lined lakes, and flat-bottomed bunkers. Other aesthetic touches include seventeen acres of hand-laid cantera stone cart paths and a seventeen-thousand-square-foot clubhouse in the Mexican Colonial style that offers views of both the Pacific Ocean and the Sea of Cortez. The developers were lucky enough to be able to hire the same manual workers who learned their craft building the Nicklaus and Jones courses nearby.

If you ever grow tired of so much *big* golf in Los Cabos, drive a few miles to Fonatur's own golf course in San Jose del Cabo. This nine-hole public layout winds through an elegant neighborhood and offers a great place to tune up your game. And the freakishly cheap green fees for eighteen holes will seem very refreshing.

In the time it's taken you to read this story, another several hundred rooms have gone up in Baja, and the government has written fourteen new press releases touting the area. So you'd better start packing before developers completely Californicate the peninsula. And if you happen to find yourself sitting at the bar of the Palmilla Hotel sipping a drink as the sky turns pink over the water, order a margarita on the rocks (no salt) for me.

9

Golf's Secret Garden

NOT FAR FROM Area 51 in the Nevada desert lies a secret as well protected as any alien spacecraft and no less unlikely. Tucked into the mountains above Boulder City thirty minutes from Las Vegas, hidden behind rocky mounds above where Highway 95 dead-ends into a road posted with signs warning not to enter, lies Cascata—a golf club so private that it has no members, a place so exclusive that the most powerful people in the golf business are afraid to talk about it. This may well be the only golf course review you ever read that doesn't describe the golf course.

To appreciate Cascata's niche in American golf requires some context. In the late 1980s, Steve Wynn, who owned the Mirage Hotel and Casino, built Shadow Creek Golf Club on a flat piece of desert wasteland outside Vegas. Tom Fazio, who designed the course, has said that Wynn gave him an unlimited budget and he exceeded it. Shadow is an utter miracle of beauty, ingenuity, and excess, a shady, creek-lined oasis of Carolinaesque golf holes that caper through a lovely and entirely man-made topography.

Since opening in 1989, Shadow Creek has provided presidents and sports heroes, entertainers and some of the richest gamblers in the world with a private enclave. Just as some casinos use deluxe suites, free meals, and front-row show tickets to entice high rollers, Wynn marketed his golf course to attract folks who might do whatever was necessary to play golf at a place that would dare exclude them. To garner an invitation to Shadow Creek you had to stay—and gamble—at the Mirage. Wynn reasoned that his guests would spend enough money in his casinos to offset the expense of operating the course. The mystique surrounding Shadow grew to Tiger Woodsian proportions.

Still, a non-revenue-producing golf course in the middle of the desert can get expensive, no matter how many sheiks and movie stars roll dice in your casino. After operating at what several industry insiders suggest was a huge deficit, Shadow began offering tee times to Mirage guests willing to pony up five hundred dollars for the pleasure of being driven to the course in a limo and whacking golf balls in the lush grass beside the artificial creek. Maybe they'd catch a glimpse of Michael Jordan in the clubhouse, or see former president Bush fishing in the pond along the third fairway.

Despite Shadow Creek's unexpected democratization, several years ago MGM decided to build an ultraprivate course to rival Shadow and possibly win over some high-rolling devotees of its own. MGM hired course architect Rees Jones to design a stunning high-budget venue (for a price tag rumored at upward of fifty million dollars) with huge elevation changes and dramatic water features in the desert outside Boulder City. But before crews finished building the place, MGM bought the Mirage. Faced with owning two non-revenue-producing golf courses that cost a gazillion dollars, MGM sold off Cascata to Park Place Entertainment (PPE), a publicly traded New Jersey gaming company that owns Caesar's Palace and other casino properties.

It doesn't require a degree in rocket science to recognize that the golf industry is fueled by hype. A continuous deluge of press releases and ads touts fantastic new "links" courses a thousand miles from the ocean, designer layouts architected by formerly great players, and themed venues that claim to re-create the windy ambience of Scotland in central Florida. Every month or two, a number of magazines crank out fluffy feature stories describing the best courses recently visited by writers who've been regaled with logoed golf shirts and sushi buffets and buckets of single-malt Scotch.

Yet Cascata opened quietly without issuing a single page of flowery prose, and without a journalist in sight. They staged no gala full of waltzing demi-dignitaries. The club's phone number remains unlisted. In fact, Park Place Entertainment has rebuffed all press requests to see the course, claiming they're just not ready for publicity. They have essentially waged an anti-marketing campaign.

Failing to receive any kind of entrée to Cascata through corporate and PR channels, I tried to talk my way in as a potential client. Surely they must have potential clients, I reasoned. So I called Caesar's Palace and identified myself as a gambler who was coming to Vegas (I *was* coming to Vegas) and wondering what it might take to play a round of golf at Cascata. A series of phone transfers eventually landed me on the line with a senior credit executive, who deflected my inquires by saying that Cascata carried "a high criteria." I implied that this wouldn't pose a problem, and asked if he could be a little more specific. He hesitantly suggested that I might, for example, want to open a casino line of credit for twenty-five thousand dollars and gamble with that money. But a hundred thousand might better ensure my invitation. He was kind enough to add that I should only gamble at a level I was comfortable with. "Why blow twenty-five thousand dollars for a round of golf?" he asked.

Unable to gather much more information about the golf course itself, I called architect Rees Jones's office, figuring that the designer of such a purportedly fabulous venue would want to talk about his work. When I told Jones's assistant what I was after she laughed good-naturedly and wished me luck. Jones himself, known for his media accessibility, said, "They're being very private about this. I don't know if I'm supposed to talk to you. I'm probably in trouble already."

But after receiving "clearance" from PPE, Jones was able to offer a few words about Cascata. "It's the eighth wonder of the golf world that they considered building a golf course on that site," he said. "We made our own soil, blasted rock, re-created streams—it was a phenomenal undertaking. You can't imagine. I can tell you everything, but no matter how I pump it up, it will actually exceed what I tell you. You have to see it."

A week later, in Vegas on other business, I tried to do just that. I pulled off the highway at Boulder City, turned left past the PRIVATE: DO NOT ENTER sign, and eventually came to a lonely gate erected as if it could hold the desert at bay. First, I rang the buzzer and asked the voice that answered if I could just come in and have a look around. He told me: sorry, no. So I climbed out of my car and walked around the gate on a rocky hill from the top of which I could see Cascata's sprawling clubhouse in the distance and a line of palms I knew defined Jones's artistry. But not wanting to be spotted, I circled back around on a dirt road that ended close to where the course lay. As I prepared for a short cross-country hike, a shiny truck with the Cascata logo drove up to the other side of the padlocked fence where I'd parked.

"Can I help you?" asked a security guard who was clearly not there to help me.

"I was looking for a place to hike."

"This is private property," he said, rattling the fence with both hands as if strangling it.

Rebuffed, I drove back toward town and stopped at the Rebel mini mart half a mile from Cascata's entrance. As I paid for my coffee I asked the cashier if she knew anything about the new golf course up the road.

"Not much. I know they're taking applications."

"For membership?" I asked, surprised.

She looked at me strangely. "For maintenance jobs. They're pay-ing twelve dollars an hour! Just drive up and they'll buzz you in."

Too late for that, and short the hundred-thousand-dollar credit line, I was even more curious about whether Cascata was really good enough to warrant this thick blanket of protection. I sought some-one who'd been to the property and was willing to talk about it—a goal tougher than sinking a long birdie putt on a slopey, three-tiered green.

My search eventually led me to Gary Galyean, architecture edi-tor at *GOLF Magazine*. Galyean was lucky enough to have visited Cascata before Park Place bought the course and dropped the cone of silence. He described "massive, striking views across miles and miles of desert, a course that grows more dramatic as it climbs. The scale is flabbergasting. It's very, very good from all the criteria you could think of: shot values, setting, playability. It has all that. And the water features are remarkable."

But Galyean also talked about the context of the new course. "There's certainly a contrast with golf in Scotland, which is like baseball here—everyone gets access. But in America we've confused that and made golf more exclusive. I don't dispute anyone's right to do that, but Cascata is just the most magnified extension of that trend. As a marketing device it will probably be very effective. If you owned a Monet and said 'I'm the only one I want to look at this,' as soon as you say that everyone wants to see it."

I also tracked down two other golfers who'd played Cascata, but who each had a vested interest in playing down how good the lay-out might be. One told me that the course was too easy and noth-ing special. The other claimed Cascata was so penal that few golfers would be willing to sustain a second thrashing. Their comments seemed to say more about how threatened they were by Cascata than about the venue itself.

Course quality and marketing strategies aside, could Cascata possibly make financial sense? When I asked the only PPE executive who returned my calls how the company could justify such an expenditure, he suggested that the gambling clientele Cascata targeted would more than make up for the costs. "It absolutely pencils out," the fellow from corporate marketing (an oxymoron, in this case) said. "We're talking about *very* high-end players. We wouldn't spend the money if it didn't make sense and offer a fair return for our shareholders."

Although many in the gaming industry agree there's no shortage of "whales" willing to wager a hundred thousand dollars or far more, at least one well-connected insider—who insisted on anonymity—questions whether Cascata is a sound business venture. "I don't know how much you can subsidize an amenity and still have it make sense," he said. "Off the record, there's no way to justify it."

When Steve Wynn built Shadow Creek it was merely daring, visionary, eccentric, and self-aggrandizing. But when a publicly traded company spends a reputed fifty million dollars on something that by design will never generate a dollar in direct revenue while simultaneously excluding most of its own shareholders from ever enjoying the asset, that's a large excess even by Vegas standards.

By writing about Cascata here I've probably furthered the success of their anti-marketing campaign. Just by reading this story, you probably want to play golf at Cascata, too. Not just because it might be a great golf course, but precisely because you're not welcome.

10

Pioneering
Canadian Golf, Ay?

JOHN COLWELL, OUR hyper, congenial host from the Canadian Department of Tourism, floored the rental van along the gravel road until the speedometer registered well over a hundred kilometers, which—if I performed the math correctly—converted to something like 2,360 miles per hour. It was nearly dusk, and we were headed for the airstrip at Margaree on Cape Breton Island, Nova Scotia, Canada. We needed to catch an airplane before nightfall.

Huddled alongside me on the van floor were my good friends Tom Liszewski and Dave Giammatteo, owners of Golf Vacations, a golf travel company in Boston. They'd invited me to accompany them on this remote scouting mission to determine whether Nova Scotia might prove an appropriate place to send clients who sought an uncrowded and unusual golf destination. Also along, and sitting comfortably in the back of the van as if we were safely parked in his driveway, was Gerry Walsh, a regular client of Tom's and Dave's.

In a bit of irony that I noticed immediately, John Colwell decelerated as soon as we hit pavement, and eventually brought the vehicle to a stop beside an eight-seat Navajo Chieftain airplane, in which two pilots from Prince Edward Air awaited us. Having sat on quite a few runways over the years hoping to take off soon enough to catch various connecting flights, I liked the idea that we'd kept our pilots waiting. As soon as it seemed safe to move, we loaded our bags and ourselves from the van into the airplane, taxied down the short runway, and took off into the darkening sky: not bound for some political summit meeting or family emergency or shareholder's conference, but en route to another golf course.

I am not advocating that most golfers travel this way. Playing eighty-seven holes of golf on seven different courses on two islands by taking six flights in three days aboard a plane the size of a love seat with wings is not everyone's idea of a good time. But when you book your next golf excursion, at least give a thought to those who came before you: pioneers like us who scouted the territory in coonskin polo shirts risking fatigue, lost golf balls, lobster dinners, and stiff drinks simply to ensure that everything would be of high enough quality and that all details would be worked out well enough to eventually satisfy you. So that you never need travel this way.

Let me preface my specific descriptions of Nova Scotia's golf venues by contradicting every travel brochure and golf magazine story you've ever seen and stating clearly that: (1) you do not "have" to visit Cape Breton and Prince Edward Islands for (2) a "Scottish style" golf vacation that will (3) "challenge players of all levels" and (4) lead you to "use every club in your bag." For one thing, even a lousy golf course will challenge most players. For another, I genuinely hate several of the clubs in my bag.

But if you happen to be the type of golfer who welcomes a little adventure—if you thrive not on valet service in the bathtub, but rather on the possibility that you'll have to sleep in a tiny airplane because you came off the eighteenth green later than expected and it was too dark to fly to your next destination because the runway there isn't equipped with lights; if you believe that every golf venue is like great literature, offering its own morals and lessons; if you collect golf courses the way serious mountaineers bag peaks, then perhaps you should call Tom and Dave and ask about an adventure golf outing. On the other hand (that is, if you're a weenie), they can also minimize all danger and unpredictability by booking you a condo in Myrtle Beach.

Our Canadian golf odyssey actually began a day earlier, with our arrival on Cape Breton, which sports seven golf courses. Just before landing, our pilot—also a golfer—buzzed the Dundee Resort golf course, our first destination. Half an hour later we stood on the first tee, with gorgeous views of Lake Bras D'Or at our backs. Appropriate to its remote location, Dundee exudes a rugged mountain character; a blue-tee slope of 135, seven water holes, plenty of thick woods, and no shortage of fairway bunkers add to the fun. And because many of Dundee's holes climb and descend like the stair-steps of an escalator, the course challenges golfers to select the right club for, say, an approach of 170 yards that plays steeply uphill over thick grass to an elevated tee in heavy air. A four-iron? A five-wood? You are wrong, Moose-breath! The correct answer: a three-wood.

At one point during this round, it occurred to me that proper club selection might require a golfer to convert from the American system to the Canadian metric system, because just about everything else involving numbers in Canada calls for applying some complex formula. For example, at the bar at the Dundee Resort I bought a Labatt's beer for three dollars. When I handed the bartender an American twenty, she gave me twenty-five dollars Canadian in change, which seemed like a very good deal. The advantageous exchange rate not only stretches your dollar, but also allows even a thirty handicap to shoot in the seventies. All of which hints at the greatest advantage of foreign travel: You can feign to understand only as much as proves convenient.

After playing Dundee's back nine at six the next morning, when the air was still and clear and mist burned off the lake and the world seemed a beautiful place to reside, we drove the much-touted Cabot

Trail to Ingonish, home of the Highlands Links. Designed by Stanley Thompson (Canada's answer to Donald Ross), this layout characterizes the shift from penal to strategic golf courses that occurred half a century ago. Holes at Highlands feature a roguish character and funny names. The course plays a solid 6,200 yards from the whites and 6,600 yards from the blues, but is even longer on great views of wooded highlands, steep bluffs, and the Atlantic Ocean.

Although the first few holes are forgettable, Highlands transforms into another golf course when the sixth emerges from flat woodlands and drops into wetlands and marshes. This 482-yard par five taunts you to go for the green in two, but water of every variety glints close by on every shot. Holes seven through twelve play through a steep gorge exploding with pink and purple lupines and sliced by a clear shallow brook running over smooth stones. The walk between twelve and thirteen (no motorized carts are available!) provides plenty of time for contemplation. But we had no such luxury, because a plane was waiting to fly us to Prince Edward Island, home of eleven golf layouts. We took off in copper light and flew through thunder and lightning and gathering dark, and the plane skidded like a shanked wedge shot. Approaching PEI, though, the cloud cover broke to reveal glittering water and pastoral views. Looking out his window at the huge arc of a rainbow hanging above one of three more golf courses we flew over, Gerry Walsh turned to me and said, "I'm so happy I could give milk."

In the morning, even after a pounding rainstorm, the Links at Crowbush Cove had absorbed nearly all the precipitation, and the cross-cut fairways glistened with the last droplets evaporating in sun and salt breezes. Whereas golf courses from Miami to Michigan tout their "linkslike" character, Crowbush Cove actually is a links—built upon seaside dunes and hillocks covered in beach grasses. With ocean views from every hole and fairways defined by tall grasses rippling in the wind like silk, this course rivals the best layouts along the entire eastern part of North America.

Crowbush plays from 4,900 to 6,900 yards; individual holes range from 87 to 603 yards. Number 2, a 296-yard par four, brims with fairway and greenside bunkers; the fifth is a rare par five awarded the number one handicap. Every moment at Crowbush is a distinct, almost illicit pleasure. The single drawback—and Tom Liszewski made note of this, and even mentioned it to the head pro—was the complete and utter lack of hot dogs.

But why complain when the awesome 6,500-yard Brudenell River Golf Course awaits? With six par threes, six par fours, and six par fives, sand traps filled with red-hued island soil, and several holes unraveling beside the hugely wide Brudenell River, the course will satisfy you far more than an overcooked wiener. The par-three tenth hole, which tees from a floss-thin strip of land out in the river and plays over water nearly all the way to the green, was one of my favorites. But it was difficult to pick just one on this great layout.

Even in Nova Scotia it eventually gets dark, so we had to wait until morning to play nine holes at the unpretentious Rustico Resort, which offers perhaps the most generous golf package in our hemisphere: three nights' lodging (in somewhat depressing motel units), three modest breakfasts, unlimited play on the short (5,900 yards) fun golf course, all the ocean views you can drink in, and a round at nearby Crowbush Cove, Brudenell, or other course, all for (at that time) $149 Canadian, which equals about forty cents U.S. Rustico's golf holes are named after Canada's eighteen prime ministers, but since the nation was currently on its nineteenth, suggestions are welcome.

After shooting a near personal-best nine at Rustico and still losing by five strokes (nine strokes Canadian) to Gerry Walsh, we traveled overland to Green Gables Golf Course, another Stanley Thompson layout built in 1939. A red fox greeted us on the first tee and politely inquired as to whether we had any extra chocolate; the front nine was equally as welcoming. Although Green Gables seemed a fine layout, it wasn't particularly memorable—perhaps because I actually continued to play well and forgot to notice details.

From Green Gables, where Gerry continued to defy his fourteen handicap by shooting one over par while blindfolded and only using one arm, we motored on to play a final nine at Summerside Golf Club, a pastoral layout that hosts the Canadian Senior Ladies Championship, which Gerry proceeded to win. Another easy course with an easygoing and delightful pro, Summerside is barely a Yonex drive from the airstrip we flew out of. I was especially fond of the finishing hole because I sank a fifty-foot putt to not lose a rather competitive match, after the other players had virtually walked off the green. Because we had another plane to catch—this one to bear us unhappily homeward.

Assuming Tom and Dave have caught up on their sleep by now, they're probably ready to send golfers off to Nova Scotia, and in all likelihood, your trip would bear few similarities to ours. Except, of course, for the good parts. When you call them, be sure to ask if Gerry is available, and try to get him as your partner.

11

Just Deserts

. . . it seems to me that the strangeness and wonder of existence are emphasized here, in the desert, by the comparative sparsity of the flora and fauna: life not crowded upon life as in other places but scattered abroad in spareness and simplicity, with a generous gift of space for each herb and bush and tree, each stem of grass, so that the living organism stands out bold and brave and vivid against the lifeless sand and barren rock. The extreme clarity of the desert light is equaled by the extreme individuation of desert life-forms. Love flowers best in openness and freedom. —EDWARD   ABBEY, *Desert Solitaire*

IF YOU'VE EVER played golf in Arizona or Southern California late in the day, when the heat begins to relent toward coolness and the air grows clear and quenching as a cold bottle of Corona with a fresh lime jammed in the neck, and the sky purples into evening, you know there's just something about the desert. Something thirsty and mysterious. Something you can't quite get your hands around (at least partly because everything's so *sharp*). Things just seem somehow more poignant in this harsh and unforgiving and inexplicably beautiful terrain. You can practically hear the drama in that familiar desert serenade: the roadrunner's plaintive *mee-meep.*

On one such afternoon several years ago, I was enjoying a solitary round of golf just before dusk on Tom Fazio's Mountain Course at Ventana Canyon, in Tucson. The day had been hot as habaneros, and I could practically feel the sun sucking the moisture from my pores as if drinking it through a straw. At 6 P.M., nobody else with a whit of sense was out anywhere: I had the golf holes and the rattlesnakes and the scorpions to myself.

As I walked toward a tee shot that had somehow found the fairway, two javelinas shuffled out of the desert and stood in the lush grass staring at me and—I'm certain—smiling. Did they wish to play through? I gazed back trying to comprehend their amusement until they eventually trotted off into the dust, no doubt having more important places to go. I looked up, as if to acknowledge a phantom gallery, but saw only saguaros shrugging their arms as if to say— sharply—"Hey; leave us out of this."

Even the word *desert* (not just a coincidence that a single letter differentiates it from *dessert*) may conjure disparate images. Some hear it and picture Saharan dunes (a good name for a country club), spitting camels, and the golf venues of Morocco, such as the Royal Courses of Mohammedia and Marrakech, and Dar es Salaam. To others it elicits the redrock canyon country of the American Southwest: Utah's Moab Golf Club; The Cliffs at Tamarron, outside Durango, Colorado; Pinon Hills, in Farmington, New Mexico; or any of dozens of great designs rolling across the dry topography around Phoenix, Tucson, and Vegas (Troon North, La Paloma, Grayhawk, Rio Secco). Still others will recall the high deserts of eastern Oregon and Washington, with their ponderosa pine and juniper companionship, a hint of sage on the breeze, black volcanic peaks sharp against the clear blue sky (like at Sunriver Resort, Broken Top, and Desert Canyon). Some will envision oasis deserts, with coconut palms and fruity rum drinks, like on the dry side of

Hawaiian Islands (Hapuna or Mauna Kea), or the oceanside cactus garden deserts of Baja (Cabo del Sol, Melia Cabo Real). The cynical among us may even think of cultural deserts, such as Miami or Minnesota, which feature more precipitation but equally fine golf.

Perhaps we love deserts for their starry skies, the contrast between hot days and cool nights, the expansive views, or the way the heat shimmers, making everything dreamlike, softening the sharp edges of a place where everything wants to bite, sting, or impale. Get out and play the great desert golf courses fast, though, because some-day the climate will utter the final word in places like Scottsdale and Henderson. Soon enough the water will run dry, you'll be able to secure a tee time at Shadow Creek, and the housing will become affordable.

Maybe we love the desert simply because golf balls fly farther there. Whatever your own reasons—and there are as many to choose from as there are varieties of bizarre flora (teddy bear and jumping cholla, barrel and fishhook cacti; boojum trees and jimsonweed; cliffrose, yucca, ocotillo)—please, just don't ever *ever* tell me, when the thermometer climbs past 118 degrees, that at least it's a dry heat.

12

Whistler's (a) Mother

ON A FOUR-DAY weekend crammed with a steep mountain ascent, long drives on murderously twisty, rain-slick highways at night, and some of the planet's sickest mountain biking, the most dangerous thing I did was play golf with my friend Bill. While I was temporarily partnered with him at British Columbia's Chateau Whistler Golf Club, Bill hit a screaming banana ball that sprang off his clubface like a scud missile. I saw it coming, but as I ran for my life on the soft grass, the ball tracked me and delivered its payload to my thigh. On the positive side, my leg deflected Bill's Titleist away from the woods and back onto the fairway. But despite my inadvertent dedication to team, my pard still made quadruple bogey on the hole.

Four of us had traveled to northwestern Canada's superlative Whistler Resort in mid-October, when even a short visit will lead any unimpaired person to jettison career, abandon family, and relocate to this killer mountain town. Days were crisp and leaf-scattered, and the cold nights presaged approaching winter at the continent's most ass-kicking ski resort. I was venturing in the company of good friends Bill Snyder, Dave Kleiber, and John Hayden, whose levels of social consciousness are exceeded only by their golf handicaps. Bill is a quirky, laser-sharp Microsoft lifer with an appetite for adventure; Dave, who manages Cascadia Revolving Fund, a nonprofit community development fund in Seattle, represented our lone family man and Packers fan; and John, a former corporate guy and current hip entrepreneur (www.jamtown.com—I promised him a shameless plug), is my frequent golf and travel partner. We aimed to pack in as much end-of-season sports fun as we could take by staging our own triathlon consisting of climbing the daunting Stawamus Chief, mountain biking, and playing four golf courses that convey major bragging rights.

To begin, we drove north from Seattle to our first destination, the two-thousand-foot vertical stone skyscraper outside Squamish, B.C., affectionately known as The Chief. As huge honkin' walls of granite go, The Chief is second only to the Rock of Gibraltar in size, and is one of Canada's top climbing destinations. Two hundred eighty routes ranging from novice to the most difficult in the entire country offer bolted sports climbs, friction challenges, incredible slabs, and other weird climbing terms.

Although cadres of young, irrational people ascend The Chief straight up its slick face while dangling from ropes, and though the four of us had summited some serious alpine peaks together in the past, we attacked The Chief via one of three "trails"—in this instance the word *trail* meaning 1.4 gazillion vertical stone and log steps hacked up the back side of the monolith. We climbed through rocky chutes full of fir and cedar, huffing past waterfalls and clear streams and sucking down doughnut-sweet air. We clomped upward over boulders, stumps, and the heaped bodies of dead Sherpas. Like any true adventurers, we toted a graphite driver and a pocketful of golf balls because this is a golf story, after all.

From the summit, our view down the steep valley was vertiginous. A sky-blue fjord shimmered below us between stands of majestic trees; in the distance, glaciers hung glittering between granite peaks. It was the most stunning natural tee box I'd ever seen.

In a rare display of decorum, the others declined to hit balls out at the lumber mill far below. I teed one up and announced that this shot was for my father, who was recovering from surgery and hoping to play his beloved game of golf again. I hauled off and shanked the ball, nearly killing an elderly couple who'd just summited. I was disappointed until I realized this was exactly the kind of shot my dad might have hit, so I immediately felt closer to him.

We stood atop The Chief for half an hour, sipping mountains and trying to catch our breath. Going down, of course, is always tougher than climbing, and by the time we reached Bill's condo at the Whistler Resort late that afternoon, we could barely hoof it up the front steps, which is exactly how you want to feel the evening before a life-threatening bike ride.

The next morning broke chilly and clear. We rented mountain bikes and warmed up on Whistler's Valley Trail—thirty kilometers of pavement that careens through woods and housing developments, past several golf courses and a scattering of lakes. The route is perfect for families (or pussy-boys) who crave a frontcountry cruise. We, however, were after something more manly: trails on which we could seriously hurt ourselves.

Toward that end, we might have opted to accompany our bikes up the ski gondola on Whistler/Blackcomb Mountain, from where cyclists can ride the well-designed mountain bike park, descend along downhill ski runs, test their medical insurance on the World Cup Course, or traverse back down on gently contoured gravel roads. In the bike park, experts duel such obstacles as teeter-totters, stumps, cable spools, and thin rails suspended between logs, and practice such moves as "bunny hops" and "nose wheelies." The downhill runs are like slalom courses on wheels, where guys like us are likely to encounter roots, sand, rocks, and other natural obstacles that would help us practice such moves as face plants and launching ourselves over our handlebars.

Off-mountain, Whistler is home to some of the gnarliest and most technical single-track biking terrain in North America, to which we shouted, "Bring it *on!*" Where else can you explore routes with names such as "Thrill Me, Kill Me," and "Moss in Your Crack"?

Whistler's toughest trails are tough in two ways—cardiovascularly and technically. All are rated like ski slopes in both categories from novice (green circles) to expert (double black diamonds). Most of the area's single-track is rated for intermediate and advanced riders, to which we whispered, "Um . . . er . . . bring it on?"

Let me just say that a "trail"—in this case *trail* meaning, essentially, "dense woods"—called "Shit Happens" disabused me of the notion that riding a bicycle is generally faster than walking. Here, it mostly *was* walking. During the occasional ten yards where we actually pedaled, our bikes administered frequent smack-downs. We spent half an hour spitting dirt and searching for the "trail" before realizing we were on it. When we humped our way back to the road on a "shortcut" called "No Girlie Man," we all thought, *Aren't Canadians funny in a mischievous and evil way.* Standing on pavement again, I noticed a bloody gash on my calf that looked, coincidentally, just like the razor-sharp edges of my pedals.

So we set off to find some terrain that Bill claimed to have "ridden" during a previous visit. Bart's Dark Trail proved a stuntman's holiday of narrow logs set across streams, and tangles of tree roots certain to bring to mind the phrase *reconstructive facial surgery.* Okay, I'm exaggerating—we were actually able to ride stretches of Bart's, and most of a mystical route called "A River Runs Through It," which ranks as an intermediate physical challenge and an advanced technical ride full of twists and loops through a beautiful, dark forest. A local mountain biking map put the trail's challenges into perspective thus: "Ask yourself the following questions: 'Can I ride a perfectly straight line for 20 metres? Can I release from my pedals while upside down in a cold, rushing creek? Can I swim? Do I have medical insurance? Is anyone looking?' If the answer to all of these questions is yes, then go for it."

Which we did, riding until we bled (actually, *that* happened pretty early on). At twilight, we performed our first sensible act of the day: ordered a pizza back at the condo and played euchre and drank a bottle of Scotch to ensure that we'd be at our absolute best for golf in the A.M.

The next morning, we arrived at the 6,397-yard Arnold Palmer–designed Whistler Golf Club in a cool drizzle. The course presented nine lakes to hit into, as well as two winding creeks to further make us mad. The rolling greens practically spelled *three-jack,* but the views of Whistler and Blackcomb Mountains allowed us to dream about skiing, a sport in which nobody keeps score. If you played Whistler conservatively, it shouldn't prove too tough. But who came to play conservatively?

Since we'd never agreed on formats for the four golf rounds ahead of us, we decided to let each golfer devise one betting game. Bill offhandedly mentioned that he wasn't really interested in gambling, until I threatened to take him out of this story unless he complied. Being a fiduciarily responsible fund manager, Dave feared a sour investment until I pointed out that if he was worried about losing five dollars, I'd make him pay green fees, which were being generously waived by our hosts.

Dave's game of choice was to alternate partners every six holes and play two-man best-ball Nassau for each six-hole match, everyone playing off my handicap. He wasted no time in establishing himself as the partner pariah—a role he honed all weekend. On the first tee, he stubbed his drive for our amusement. Out of sheer embarrassment we offered him a mulligan and he went on to win the hole.

We played erratically and quietly trash-talked our way around the charming layout the way only close friends can. When John and I were partnered temporarily, he executed an unforgettable shot on number seven, a 356-yard romp bisected by a stream. Rather than carrying the water and going for the green from 140 yards, he chose the unorthodox approach of topping his ball over the narrow bridge with laser precision.

"Hmm," I observed. "Most guys wouldn't have laid up here." On number thirteen, when we switched partners again, John reminded me to swing hard and lift my head.

The weather cleared and we warmed to the course's subtle Palmerisms, such as the 457-yard par-five sixteenth hole's double dare to attack the green over water on your second shot. But we all played like double weenies and were lucky to get on in four.

Upon dispensing with Palmer we were ready for Nicklaus. We sped across the village to our afternoon tee time at Nicklaus North Golf Course. John decreed that we would play "Big Kahuna"—a game of his invention—which consists of longest drive on every hole (John is six foot two and built like a Coke machine); Wolf; and closest to the pin on the par threes. The par-seventy-one, 6,413-yard track proffered generous fairways (ideal for Kahuna) lined with western-style mansions of wood, glass, and stone (ideal for shattering windows). It also provided the best views I've ever seen from a golf course, and that's exclusive of the teenage girl who inexplicably darted naked across the first fairway, a clear omen, I thought—but of what?

Nick North's user-friendly front side actually contained one water-free hole, but the lakes were mostly decorative, at least for me. However, the trees—and a particular set of ladies' tee markers—were sometimes in play. I picked up seven dots including a handful of Kahunas, my favorite of which caromed off the butt of the bear marking the ladies tee before lurching back onto the fairway—a winner since nobody else hit the short grass. Bill picked up nine dots, three earned when he went lone wolf on the 153-yard par-three sixth and made four for two. Dave and John picked up seven dots between them, and you can probably guess by now who earned the fewest.

On the back nine—which contains three par threes (two of which stretch over 200 yards), and another hole without water—Dave's strategy was to card all sevens except on two holes where birdie putts (he missed them) earned him some dots. On the 537-yard eleventh, Bill boastfully went lone wolf again and chunked two

drives into the shrubbery within kicking distance. Strolling down
the eighteenth fairway toward that stream-guarded green, I noticed
a large pile of fresh scat, which I knew was not a signature design
element executed by the Golden Bear himself.

When I pointed this out to the others, and made a joke about
outrunning such a danger, Bill said, "You can't outrun a grizzly."

"I don't need to outrun a grizzly," I replied. "I only need to outrun you."

Although I shot eighty-five and won fourteen dots overall, John
won the Big Kahuna title to my Big Chagrin.

On the final morning of our mega-athlon, we guzzled coffee and
made tracks for the Chateau Whistler Golf Club. The previous day, when
we'd told some other golfers we'd be playing Chateau Whistler, they'd
smiled sympathetically, like we were morons. We soon found out why.

The 6,635-yard Robert Trent Jones Jr. mountain layout is simply
daft. The first four holes are almost a parody. On number one, even
though Bill carded a twelve, he emerged from the woods with a
triumphant grin, claiming he'd "netted out" by finding more balls than
he'd lost. On number two, two perfectly struck approach shots and two
putts, for godsakes, rolled back off the green. On number three, a ludicrous uphill dogleg left with a blind hairpin approach over a ravine,
John's pitch from below the hole had no chance of stopping within a
dozen yards of the pin (and not just because it was John hitting). His
subsequent chip from the opposite side had no chance either.

I'd decreed that we play alternating partners and count both net
scores, low one first, so that if my partner and I shot four and five we
carded a forty-five. If our opponents shot five and six, or fifty-six, we
picked up eleven dots. A birdie reversed the digits of the opponents'
score. For the first six holes I was partnered with Dave, so of course
I lost money. On the 163-yard sixth hole, John stuck his tee shot
inches from the hole. Approaching the green I asked Bill how close
John was and he suggested I look between my legs. Dave and I lost

thirty-two dots when John's birdie reversed our thirty-five into a fifty-three.

John and I were partnered next and enjoyed some success, picking up twenty-six dots on the 184-yard eighth. And then Bill and I won 13, 40, 1, and 12 before he hit me in the thigh with his ball. I still shot a post-traumatic five by dropping a forty-foot putt on the 424-yard par four, but Dave miraculously netted a par. I won't bore you with the final tallies except to say that Bill, who won with 150 dots, earned approximately one dot for every stroke he took.

Having inflicted maximum divot carnage at Chateau Whistler, we sped twenty miles north to Big Sky Golf and Country Club, an immaculate Bob Cupp design at the foot of the sheer granite face of 8,300-foot Mount Currie. Three-hundred-sixty degree mountain views and perfectly coifed fairways characterize this layout where holes carry names such as "Purgatory" (apt) and "Tranquility" (sarcastic).

We toted hot coffee in the imminent drizzle. Although we feared Bill would call "no trump," he agreed to play skins if we gave him three strokes on the par fives and two on the rest. Worn down by arguing and computing scores, we assented. Bill blew a chance to win three skins on the 177-yard third hole by yanking a two-foot putt, and we gleefully uttered the Homer Simpson *"doke!"* sound. I fell in love with the fourth hole, a 520-yard hottie with a curvaceous stream dicing the perfect fairway into four landing areas. Bill quieted us on the short fifth hole by making a double bogey for par and winning five skinnies, which still doesn't seem right. Despite his radical inconsistency, Bill could play golf every couple of holes or so, and we'd made the mistake of taking him out for enough rounds that he was developing a game. Dave, on the other hand, showed little improvement, though we continued to like him nonetheless.

On the seventh hole, rain began falling in earnest. We donned fleece and Gore-Tex, and puffed cigars against the chill, but were happy to quit after nine to add a fourth event to our triathlon: the burger-eating contest, which we took to with relish, and were able to participate in without betting on the outcome.

13

Old Works, New Tricks:

Turning a Superfund Site into a Super-Fun Golf Course

YOU'D BE HARD-PRESSED to find a town in America or in any other first-world nation as bleak and disheartening as Butte, Montana, a place that has literally digested itself. A place that other Montanans like to refer to by dropping the final *e*. In the atrophied, arsenic-laden heart of Butte, lovely brick Victorians crumble behind plywood, and once-grand hotels bustle only with spiders and wheezing ghosts. Drive about a mile out from the formerly stately main drag, and dirt roads will lead you right up to the precipitous edge of the most horrifically impressive abandoned open-pit copper mine in the galaxy. The bleeding orange hole gapes a mile and a half wide and two thousand feet deep and is filled with a cocktail so toxic that a mad scientist couldn't have devised such a recipe. On the bluffs above the massive hole, the wind blows cold and lonely. Along descending, artificially gouged mesas, old mining apparati still hunch above abandoned mine shafts like iron tyrannosaurs devouring the earth.

The nearby town of Anaconda—where the Copper Kings built a series of smelters to process Butte's ore—isn't much cheerier. It exudes the same downbeat, kick-me ambience, but lacks Butte's former grandeur—although Anaconda *is* home to what was once the tallest smokestack in the world. After environmental problems closed the mines and hence the smelters back in the 1980s, *The New York Times* referred to Anaconda as "a company town without the company."

Visiting these hard-luck Hootervilles makes you wish to drop a stadium-sized Prozac tablet on the entirety of Deer Lodge County. Unless you're drawn to tragedy or have to pee so badly that you can't speed past the forlorn exit on Interstate 90, only one thing could possibly draw you to Anaconda, Montana; only one sprig of both literal and metaphorical greenery barks out from among the hangdog grays and blacks: The town happens to boast an utterly anomalous and ridiculously inexpensive Jack Nicklaus signature golf course, which happens to be located atop a former EPA Superfund site.

In 1883 "Copper King" Marcus Daly erected the upper works of a huge smelting operation in Anaconda to handle ore coming out of nearby Butte—four billion tons valued at twenty-two billion dollars over the next hundred years. A second lower works followed the original in 1887. Business boomed heartily enough that in the early twentieth century, Daly replaced the old works with the spanking-new Washoe Smelter, which boasted the world's highest smokestack, rising sixty stories above the Montana foothills, a dark, coughing symbol of a certain kind of prosperity. Anaconda's smelters continued to belch out the smoke that locals equated with good times for another half century. Then, in the 1970s, when Chile nationalized its mines (thus throwing out the American copper rascals) and U.S. air pollution standards conspired to make extraction a tough business, Anaconda Copper Mining Company began divesting its Montana holdings. It sold the Anaconda facility to ARCO in 1977, and ARCO closed the works three years later. Three years after that the EPA listed the smelter as a Superfund site, sticking ARCO with the bill for a century of environmental roguery.

ARCO's cheapest option was to throw a blanket over the waste and fence in the whole poisonous gulag—a solution that didn't much please locals in this town of ten thousand, hundreds of whom were recently unemployed. As so often happens in such situations, ARCO decided not to decide anything for several years, during which the Butte-Anaconda area slipped farther down the slag heap.

Then in 1989 a city councilman named Gene Vucovich was struck by a wacky idea. Driving through Coeur D'Alene, Idaho, he noticed a golf course built on the site of an old sawmill. Why not dare similar irreverence at the Old Works site, he reasoned to fellow council members, who enjoyed a good laugh at his expense.

Five years later, though, Vucovich's dream acquired some bulk: a team consisting of ARCO, the town of Anaconda, the EPA, Deer Lodge County, and the Montana Department of Health and Environmental Services roped together to scale a mountain of regulations and try to build a golf course on the Anaconda smelter site. They brought in Jack Nicklaus to design the thing, figuring they needed a high-profile architect to make this elephant fly. When Nicklaus showed up on a scouting mission he was received like an astronaut by cheering crowds and high-school baton twirlers. In a refreshing respite from the usual PR hype, Nicklaus described the Old Works site as "one of the ugliest properties I have ever seen."

Instead of spending an estimated $65 million to haul away Anaconda's smelter pollution (and where would they put it, anyway?), ARCO ponied up $30 million in remediation costs and another $11 million (including $1 million to Nicklaus) to construct a very strange golf course above the entire mess.

The engineering challenges posed by building Old Works were as monumental as the paperwork. Crews covered the smelter wastes—which stood as deep as eight feet in places—with a two-inch layer of lime, more than a foot of clay, and ten inches of dirt and sand, which they then seeded with grass. Greens, tees, bunkers, and lakes were underlined with PVC plastic to prevent moisture from percolating down into the waste and discharging into streams. The complex drainage system had to ensure that excess water would be captured in artificial lakes rather than entering natural systems. And when grounds crews dig for any reason, they must save out, separate, and then replace materials in precise layers. All told, construction crews pushed around 1.3 million cubic yards of dirt. When the whole thing was finished, developers turned ownership of the Old Works Golf Course over to the town of Anaconda, making it the world's most expensive Jack Nicklaus signature muni owned by a bunch of unemployed smelter workers.

The result of these astounding efforts is a beautiful and bizarre golf venue on the outer fringe of the middle of nowhere. The design neatly incorporates elements from the old smelter works: Enormous iron ladles now spilling only wildflowers greet players on their way to the first tee. Granite slabs from the mill line the banks of Warm Springs Creek and protect the tenth green. Old smelter furnaces border the third fairway, and a 150-foot flue backdrops the par-three fourth hole. Throughout the course, glimmering black slag heaps provide contours, and rocks rendered green by the smelting process mark the lines between generous fairways and gently waving fescues. As a final touch, Nicklaus filled all the bunkers with powdery black slag.

Five sets of tees—named brick, limestone, copper, gold, and slag—reinforce the mining heritage of this 7,705-yard track. Individual holes bear such monikers as Black Canyon, Refiner, Slum House, and Copper Kings. Across a landscape where formerly no living thing dared to tread, now deer, elk, marmots, and even mountain lions stroll across fairways and search for lost balls in the high grass. Though long and hilly still, the previously toxic topography makes for a fine walk. It is a formidable and wondrous course.

With a high-season rate of thirty-eight dollars, Old Works has been called the most affordable Jack Nicklaus championship layout in the world. Many locals pay $625 annually to belong to a club they otherwise could not have even dreamed of living within five hundred miles of. Outside the golf business, everyone from industry bigwigs to Sierra Clubbers have praised this innovative project. Who wouldn't love to see a golf course grow up through a blighted waste dump?

Still, one question haunts Old Works the way the legacy of black-lung disease still clings to the town of Anaconda: Is this really as good an idea as it seems?

The nearest major city to Anaconda (Salt Lake) lies a full day's drive away. And though Montana is the fourth largest state, its population crests at just under nine hundred thousand souls. The population of Deer Lodge County, in particular, has declined by nearly half over the past forty years. Boosters point out that two million tourists pass close by on Interstate 90 on their way to Glacier and Yellowstone National Parks each summer, but how many can be counted on to stop in for a round of golf?

In small towns throughout the West, circumstances are forcing formerly extractive economies—especially those erected on mining and timber—to try morphing into tourist draws, begging the question of whether unemployed miners and loggers will serve scones to bed-and-breakfast guests or willingly man the pro shop desk. While the Old Works Golf Course employs a few dozen workers for about seven months each year, it has not yet drawn a reliable stream of tourists to the area. It has not inspired a major corporation to build a hotel.

Now that the town of Anaconda owns the former Superfund site, locals are responsible for making the golf course that's built upon it succeed, and by all indications they're off to a fine start. And sure, they'll benefit from any surplus cash (the course is designated a nonprofit entity and must turn excess revenue over to the county). But they'll also be accountable if Old Works fails to generate enough money to cover maintenance and operations once the half-life of hype exerts its influence. And if any serious environmental problems occur in the future, the people of Anaconda can no longer hit up a deep-pocketed corporation to make things right. Which is to say that while everyone who believes in justice and resurrection is rooting for Old Works, it's still in some ways a western-style saloon gamble, the losing side of which could turn the place into a ghost town—although a greener one—again.

14

Locals Rule:

The Sure Bet of Las Vegas Golf

EVERY STORY ABOUT Las Vegas should feature a blackjack dealer named Dino who's built like a bull terrier and growls in a voice rough with stogies and Johnny Walker Black. I met my Dino on the first tee of the Lakes Course at Primm Valley Golf Club, a forty-minute cruise from the strip. After knocking his tee shot into a steep fairway bunker, Dino said to his Warbird, "You, Mister, are headed for the penalty box"—an area in his golf bag reserved for misbehaving clubs. By the looks of his bag Dino's Callaways had been racketeering, so they felt right at home in Vegas, a city whose cast of characters comes right out of a police line-up. At one point, when I asked Dino what hole we were on and he said, "number three," our other two playing partners stepped forward.

Of course, only locals really experience the shadowy underside of this city that can be anything visitors want it to be: smooth and classy as Sinatra, glitzy as KISS, hotter than a lap dance, solidly respectable as . . . well okay, maybe not solidly respectable. You want Paris? Venice? Pirate ship? Pyramid? Yeah, they got that. But the best way to find the best of Vegas is to learn what the dealers and caddies and cocktail waitresses prefer. After all, for whatever twisted reason, they live here.

Although my new pal Dino claimed he wasn't a gambler, he took some long-shot chances on Primm Valley's cheerful 6,945-yard Lakes layout, designed by Tom Fazio. The course features an extensive lake and river system set against the backdrop of the Sierra Nevada Mountains. Fazio moved mountains himself in constructing valleys of natural sand and an actual oasis. The course features small, tiered greens and plentiful steep, severe, yet fluffy bunkers that lend a pure feel. While the holes on the Lakes Course carry names like "Cactus Springs" and "Rock Bottom," Dino invented a few names for his clubs, such as "!@#$%!" and "*^%!!!!." He filled the penalty box on the boisterous par-four fifteenth hole, which stretches 450 yards arm-in-arm with a stream. Primm is also home to Fazio's equally dandy 7,131-yard Desert Course, which plays tougher and longer amid cacti, palms, native grasses and plateaus.

As I was lining up a putt on the fourth hole of the new Bali Hai Golf Club, located at the south end of the Vegas strip, a plane flew so close overhead that the flight attendant asked me if I preferred chicken or beef. Designed by Lee Schmidt and Brian Curley, and incorporating 4,000 trees and 100,000 tropical plants and flowers, an island green and a stunning Polynesian-style clubhouse that contains a Wolfgang Puck restaurant, this 7,015-yard venue still falls short of what you'd expect from such inflated green fees. Though I may get whacked for saying so, $34.5 million didn't buy more than mediocre golf holes, though it purchased plenty of blinding white sand that you're not even allowed to play out of. Several holes here seem reminiscent of others, yet most are still forgettable. On the positive side, you could be tying your golf shoes in Bali Hai's parking lot fifteen minutes after stowing your tray table. And you'll enjoy service worthy of an emperor.

Only in Vegas can you rush from Polynesia to the British Isles just by driving across town. I headed to the Royal Links Golf Club, executed by Dye Designs, for an afternoon game with Shawn White, a floor supervisor at the Aladdin Casino. We met outside the stately

Scottish castle/clubhouse and were joined by Doug Low, one of the best caddies I've ever had the pleasure of strolling alongside. In addition to dispensing yardages and strategic advice, and describing the position of every hidden bunker on the course, Low told jokes, recommended restaurants, and shared plenty of stories that I can't repeat.

Royal Links offers a collection of replica holes from British Open courses, and a compelling yardage book that describes a great moment from each. The layout, encompassing 107 pot bunkers and overseeded to lend that bare British winter look, stretches to 7,029 yards.

We started with number ten from Royal Lytham. Shawn nearly drove the green, but his second shot, a short pitch, traveled nearly as far. When we reached the third hole, the Royal Links pro was waiting on the tee. This being Vegas, he offered us 2-1 odds on a pro-shop purchase that he could knock it closer to the pin. He won, we moved on—to holes from Troon, St. Andrews, and Prestwick. We dodged pods of invisible bunkers, and Shawn educated me about the casino business (note: the casinos usually win) as a brisk wind kicked up off the North Atlantic—or at least it felt that way.

The next morning Shawn had to teach a dice class so I was forced to make a couple of hard eights in the company of his boss, Grady Aitken. We met at the $4 billion Lake Las Vegas Resort, in Henderson. Grady called it "the place to live if money is no object." Jack Nicklaus's Reflection Bay Golf Club gave us plenty to reflect upon there: such as why are we such lousy golfers? Five holes unfurl along 1.5 miles of lakeshore. Wide fairways with great visual lines occasionally force hidden shots across these 7,261 yards of top-notch golf.

Early holes on each side climb along steep canyons before descending with dramatic views to finishing holes beside the lake. The 199-yard par-three eighth is set on a peninsula jutting into the water, and nestled among beaches, bunkers, palms, and rockwork. Eighty-one bunkers and three waterfalls gave the Wendy's Three-Tour Challenge plenty of challenge here in 1998. Several holes feature double carries over water and/or ravines.

Our companions at Reflection Bay were a couple of tough guys from back east who didn't talk much. When I asked the fellow with the black tee shirt and size-24 neck what line of work he was in, he whispered "broker." Later, when I asked his companion if he was a broker too, he said, "Waddaya mean, broker?" I left it at that. However, they were generous enough to share their sandwiches, which they'd had flown in that morning from "the best friggin' deli in New Jersey." How could I say no?

Though Grady and I embraced the good life at LLV, many locals (especially those who don't list their occupation as "gazillionaire") prefer to play at the more affordable DragonRidge Golf Club—and not just because it's a good place to bury a body. Located twenty minutes from the action, this 7,039-yard Jay Morrish/David Druzisky design hosted Tiger Jam 2000. Expansive views and dramatic elevation changes characterize a remote venue crafted out of the McCullough Mountains. The very playable course sports many directional bunkers which shouldn't worry you nearly as much as the difficult Bentgrass greens; sidehill putts are as prevalent here as cologne at a $2 craps table.

The front side is smart and handsome, but number ten blows a nine-hole winning streak. A 368-yard par four with a wash running down the center, the hole offers a choice between two options that you can't see, but what you think is a well-struck shot to either fairway might still end up in the quarry. The thirteenth hole, at 375 yards, features a tiny desert island green with a lone but dangerous pot bunker. Overall, DragonRidge doesn't breathe fire as much as it puffs magic.

Although it seems unlikely that heaven would be located anywhere close to Las Vegas (not counting a heaven-themed casino with leggy angel waitresses, roulette wheels floating atop clouds, and slots ringing with harp music), Shadow Creek Golf Club is probably a pretty accurate facsimile thereof. Once the private enclave of celebrities and high rollers, now any knucklehead with $500 (and who's staying at an MGM/Mirage property) can enjoy the most astounding example of golf and excess ever dreamed up. Architect Tom Fazio claims he was given an unlimited budget for Shadow Creek and exceeded it.

Fazio essentially manufactured an entire ecosystem, creating a rocky creek with waterfalls, a lush, rolling Carolinian landscape, and huge elevation changes on a formerly flat desert wasteland. While mystique is part of Shadow Creek's draw (you'll spot Michael Jordan's and President Bush's lockers inside) it's also one of the most sublime courses you'll probably never play.

Choose from only two sets of tees, and rely on your caddie (included—as is limousine transport—in green fees) because there are no yardage signs. You'll see few other golfers because management limits play to a max of 80 golfers daily, according to GM Mark Brenneman, who is an engaging partner in addition to running a frappe-smooth operation. Watch for exotic pheasants as you tee off beside the lovely creek. Admire the gentle bunkering and the snowy mountains in the distance.

Note the lake on the par-five third hole, where head caddie Clayton Miyata was pulled into the water by an apparently ferocious bass (we may assume he took a penalty drop and lay three when he climbed out). The fourth hole somehow plays over a pine forest (Fazio imported 21,000 mature trees). On number eight, called Shangri-La, John Daly once asked for a do-over when he missed the green. The back side opens with two short, easy feel-good holes. A few more gullies and ridged greens and drop-dead gorgeous fairways will bring you to number seventeen, a steep par-three with a tiny green lurking behind a lake and beside a jungly waterfall. Shadow Creek's timeless beauty and extraordinary ambience are likely to stay with you long after Clayton Miyata dries out from his inadvertent swim.

Hard-hitting Shawn White (who was hitting it particularly hard by heading from the casino night shift to the first tee) joined me again for a round at the well-crafted TPC Canyons Course, designed by Bobby Weed and home of the Las Vegas Senior Classic. The 7,063-yard course opens gently, by which I mean it didn't confront us with a forced carry until the second hole. By number eight, as a cold rain fell, the layout really cinched down with a 458-yard uphill par four into the wind. Shawn and I talked about lunch, soup, skipping our scheduled afternoon round. From number ten on, nearly ever single hole grew progressively tougher, with more and longer forced carries over deep arroyos. On the signature fourteenth, 365 yards over an arroyo and bunker with an approach to a green perched on the lip of another arroyo, Shawn hit his drive so hard it sounded like an F-15. Suddenly he thought maybe the weather would clear for the afternoon round after all. We were actually sorry to leave this excellent layout, but we had other rows to hoe.

When Pete Dye completes his third golf course on the windy high-desert Paiute Indian Reservation, there'll be one hole for every member of the tribe. Paiute Golf Resort's Snow Mountain course is the kinder, gentler layout, designed with pot bunkers, lakes, and the occasional flair of railroad ties. Scrubbier than most Vegas courses and featuring a staff who wouldn't even notice if you were bleeding to death in the pro shop, this 7,146-yard track has a refreshingly remote feel. Nearly every hole seems to dogleg, and many require big drives to carry various hazards. The solid course finishes with three waterside holes. Eighteen presents a 445-yard par four with a green hiding behind a skinny neck of grass between bunkers and lake. Breathe in the clean scent of sage and catch your breath before heading out on the equally perky and well-designed 7,112-yard Sun Mountain course as an encore.

Vegas locals revere the Revere at Anthem, which climbs in and out of canyons, clings to cliffs, scoots over lakes and waterfalls, and showcases the talents of architect Greg Nash. White-glove service and a state-of-the-art driving range attract all sorts of Vegasites to this Del Webb community on the outskirts of Henderson. Nash created a course with a gigantic wow factor; you might utter that word three or four times just on the 625-yard eleventh hole, which drops faster than the NASDAQ market from canyon rim tee boxes, plays over or around a desert island, and finishes at a green and bunker complex that recreates the Japanese yin-yang symbol when seen from above. Incredible water features are just the icing on the wonderful, intricate cake that is the Revere.

Cost aside, Rees Jones's Rio Secco Golf Club, near the Revere, is also fabulous as all get-out. Featuring six plateau holes, six canyon holes, and six holes winding through broad desert washes, there's no shortage of startling variety. The course stretches to 7,332 yards from the tips, and its 240 acres in the foothills of the Black Mountains encompass two acres of lakes, 92 acres of grass, and 88 traps. The rest is desert: You do the math.

Rio Secco is not for the feint of heart—or driver. Hackers will suffer here (sorry, Dino). But decent players, or those who don't care about score or lost balls (ladies and gentleman, welcome Shawn White) will rave about this excellent and unique venue. Unfortunately, the green fees will make you suffer too—and you can only pay the too-high price if you're a guest of the Rio Suites hotel.

After a small collection of forced carries, contemplate the delightful seventh hole, which begins from extremely elevated tees aimed at a visually tricky landing area. The approach is played into a natural caliche amphitheater. The tenth hole begins with a shot that must reach toward the Stratosphere (the hotel, not the cosmic zone). Number twelve will rocket your pulse rate with a required launch over a ravine so steep that the echo of your tee shot may startle the group behind you when they eventually reach the tee. Holes sixteen through eighteen play over and around blue lakes and in view of the stately clubhouse, providing a feeling that you've commenced your desert journey and returned to civilization.

At least until you drive back to Vegas.

15

When Irish Lies
Are Smiling

IF I LEARNED one thing from playing several great golf courses in Ireland, it's that not all Guinness Stout is created equal. For example, the stout poured in the clubhouse bar at the Killarney Golf and Fishing Club—which you can sip while looking down at the eighteenth green and betting on whether the guy in the gray fisherman's sweater will get down in two from in the shrubbery—may actually be far superior in temperature to the pint you get upstairs at Ballybunion on a rainy day, though the Ballybunion Guinness may very well feature a more perfect, creamier head and seem the ideal chaser to a shot of Jameson's Irish Whiskey that you imbibe purely for medicinal purposes after playing golf for four hours in a driving rain. And though the links at Waterville are among many visitors' favorite golf venues in this green and lovely and gentle country, the bartender there may, on occasion, fail to let the Guinness settle for the proper amount of time before serving it.

I earned the equivalent of a master's degree in Guinness while visiting Ireland to play in the annual Jameson Irish Whiskey International Golf Challenge—a sort of World Cup event for players with less than a twenty-eight handicap. More than two hundred golfers from nearly a dozen countries entered the event in teams of four. Each day participants are paired with one of their own team-mates and another pair of golfers from another team—and usually from another country. The competition is based on the modified Stableford scoring system with full handicaps, which is to say that, for example, a net birdie earns you three points, a net par scores two points, a net bogey collects one point, and a net double bogey incurs the wrath and disdain of your partner. At the end of each day of the tournament, scorekeepers tally up the points from the three best cards from each team of four. Prizes are awarded for most overall points, most points at each golf venue each day, most points per country, and for many other achievements. The event takes place over three days, during which golfers play at Waterville, Ballybunion, and Killarney.

I was invited to the tournament as a guest of the Irish Tourist Board and Aer Lingus, which ensured that I wouldn't take home a prize by teaming me up with another journalist, a TV anchorman, and a public relations specialist (not a short-game specialist) from the airline. Each day, after my round, I waited expectantly for my partners to show up at the bar, and each day I saw their sheepish, embarrassed faces heading straight for the bartender, after which they downed shots of Jameson's before seeking me out to deliver the bad news.

I actually arrived for the competition a day early, and drove to Killarney's Great Southern Hotel (host venue for the tournament) with Tim O'Connor, a Canadian golf journalist who was so kind that he stopped the car to help a cow get its head back under a barbed-wire fence—although the cow seemed to be enjoying the rich grass outside the fence and wasn't in any distress. Then we took in a practice round at the very new and still-uncelebrated (but not for long) Beaufort Golf Course. Tim was even so kind as to play badly enough for me to beat him, although he's a low-single-digit handicap. But Tim ultimately revealed that he'd been saving his best golf for the tournament, and I was sorry not to have him as a partner.

The weather was spotty that afternoon, and the golf course was absolutely empty, although we did encounter Irish golf legend Christie O'Connor telling stories in the bar as we warmed up with bowls of potato and leek soup. Outside, the golf course, which plays as long as 6,792 yards from the championship tees, winds among two-hundred-year-old trees on the grounds of an estate built back in 1740. While this parkland layout is scenic and challenging throughout, the holes get truly good around number eight. The ninth requires a long field goal struck between uprights formed by stately pine trees. The ruins of a twelfth-century castle distract you from the tee box of the 207-yard par-three thirteenth and remain in view for a few excellent holes that wind over sculpted mounds and dogleg here and there through the pleasing terrain. Of course, after playing well during my practice round, I developed high expectations for the tournament. I was to begin the next morning at Waterville, located halfway out the Ring of Kerry, a classic hundred-mile scenic drive punctuated by lakes, mountain passes, seascapes, quaint villages, and other attractions.

Unfortunately, my own driving wasn't nearly so classic that day, as I sprayed tee shots into many of the sand dunes and much of the gorse that create the formidable character of this layout along Ballinskellig's bay. The course, constructed around 1885, plays out onto a node of perfect, awesome linksland to as long as 7,184 yards and a slope of 141 (from the middle tees it's a far more manageable 6,549/139). Many holes stretch right along the sea and most others are still in view of it. The weather was typical Irish for October— cold sideways rain and wind so strong it made opening your umbrella a kind of adventure sport.

In many countries, there are stiff legal penalties for playing golf as poorly as I did at first, but Ireland is far too friendly a place for that. Although I hit beautifully off the practice tee, no points were awarded there. A little nervous on number one, I took no less than a ten, feeling much as if I'd burned an American flag in public. And the name of this 395-yard par-four starting hole? "Last Easy"—a bad sign. The rest of the day proved nearly as tough, and the 550-yard finishing hole lined with gorse-covered dunes made the bar look like heaven. When we went in for a bracing whiskey, golf announcer Ben Wright was sipping his own by the broad window, but I was glad to learn that he hadn't been commentating on my game.

Still, I'd recovered my composure enough on this opening day at Waterville to rack up twenty-one Stableford points and not be the guy whose card was dropped. As soon as we got back to the Great Southern Hotel that evening, I rushed to the posting board to make sure that at least a few other players had made out worse than I did. Then I sought out those fine gentlemen to talk in great detail about our rounds.

Although nothing in the tournament brochures hinted at this, there was an aspect of the Ironman competition to the Jameson event. I figured this out that first evening, as our hosts drew pint after pint of Guinness at the cozy Killeen House, where I enjoyed a fabulous lamb dinner, listened to a pub room full of Irishmen tell jokes, and admired the collection of far-flung golf balls and bag tags arranged nattily on the walls.

None of which helped to prepare me—mentally or otherwise— to wake early and drive (on the left, of all things!) through another cold rain to Ballybunion Golf Club, a course about which Tom Watson has remarked, "A man would consider that the game originated there." Tucked comfortably between the River Shannon and the Atlantic Ocean, Ballybunion is now possibly my favorite golf course on the planet—a rolling seascape of windblown grasses climbing ancient, massive dunes. Many tees and greens are located atop these dunes, and each time you climb one and look around, you see other golfers atop other dunes that protrude like islands above the sea of swaying (but vengeful) grasses.

This 6,542-yard, par-seventy-one (from the tips) layout was established in 1893, but somehow the club failed a few years later. A dedicated member got it started again in 1906, and some thirty-one years later, management brought in famous British golf course architect Tom Simpson to improve the links a bit. But Ballybunion is the kind of course where the best architect could only think to tweak a few greens and add a bunker; still, that bunker has become hugely controversial over the years. The holes here were reordered in 1971, and though Tom Watson recently added a few touches, these seem wholly gratuitous. The course was already as near to perfect as it could have been, and Tom should have simply made a few pithy remarks and gone home.

To set an appropriate mood, Ballybunion's first hole unfurls beside a graveyard full of weathered headstones. You'll need a caddie here to describe preferred positions and approaches throughout the course, even if you're not capable of following his advice. Many holes feature blind or just plain dangerous approaches between, around, or over dunes and dips and turns. The sixth hole plays out to a narrow, sloping green perched on the edge of a high cliff overlooking crashing waves. It is an awesome promontory. The eighteenth concludes with a half-blind uphill approach shot over a waste area known fondly as "Sahara." I played Ballybunion in the company of a pair of charming Irishmen who regaled me with stories, some of which I actually understood. My game improved over the previous day; I scored twenty-seven points and was not heckled at all.

On our third and last morning of competition—on the Killeen Course at the Killarney Golf and Fishing Club—the weather was, surprisingly, raining. This course plays along the island-studded Lough Leane, and offers sweeping views of the MacGillicuddy's Reeks rising from the distant shore. The parkland layout (6,006 meters, par seventy-one from the white tees) gathers far less wind than the links courses I'd been playing, but also features streams and lakes and trees. Throughout the day, the rain spit and then relented, the sun broke through and then disappeared, and I burned several thousand calories simply donning and removing my sweater and rain gear every other hole.

The course begins with a short hairpin dogleg that bends around a good fishing lake. Number three presents a tough par three of 162 meters into the wind. Then the layout turns inland and opens up a little more. I came out of the starting gate possessed—shooting par for birdie, two bogeys for pars, and par for birdie, a record-setting pace until bad luck in a water hazard beside the tiny, slippery platform green on number six led to double, triple, triple. Still, I recovered to earn Stableford points on every subsequent hole, for a total of thirty-four, just a few shy of the day's highest score. My partner shot thirty-six points, so all we needed was one more halfway decent score from one of our other partners; but they entered the bar after the round practically baa-ing out loud.

And so the competition was over, except for the always painful presentation of trophies at a gala dinner at the Great Southern Hotel. The next morning we toured the cliffs of Moher—featured in the movie *The Secret of Roan Inish*—which tower seven hundred feet above the sea for miles. Although several of us were ailing from the after-tourney party, we also headed out against all common sense to play a round at Lahinch, an incredible funhouse of a golf course first laid out by Old Tom Morris in 1893 and then transformed by Alistair Mackenzie, who modestly commented, "Lahinch will make the finest and most popular golf course ever created"—hype worthy of Disney, except he may have been right. Despite blinding hangovers, we were moved by the stone ruins, the river winding beneath a lovely bridge toward the sea, and the feeling of utter peace and beauty. Two holes on the front nine alone feature blind shots over mountainous dunes—like playing golf by Braille.

On our last night in Ireland, our hosts afforded us the immense luxury of staying at the five-star Adare Manor. For several centuries this stone castle, set on 840 acres, was home to the earl of Dunraven, who must have lost either his senses or his fortune to have sold it. Sixty-four palatial, high-ceilinged rooms look out over formal gardens, winding streams, gorgeous green lawns, and a new Robert Trent Jones golf layout. It made for a fitting end to a royal golf trip.

16

From Slopes to Slope Ratings

In which one writer asks the question: Is it worth the effort to ski and play golf on the same long weekend? The answer won't surprise you.

IT TOOK ME two trips to load all the gear from my car onto the airport parking lot shuttle: golf clubs, skis and poles, boot bag, airplane carry-on, and a suitcase and duffel bag containing everything from shorts and golf polos, to long underwear and ski goggles, to a couple of shirts to wear in the evenings.

As I finally took my seat, a guy with a wafer-thin briefcase and a pair of expensive shoes remarked sarcastically, "Looks like a tough trip."

Actually, he had no idea.

In spring, when most folks are trading in their skis for golf clubs, I find myself having trouble letting go. Although I can barely wait to feel that delicious *thwok* of driver against golf ball after laying off all winter, I'm still reluctant to abandon the equally distinct pleasure of carving turns in knee-deep powder. This year I thought: Why not ease through the difficult transition by visiting a place where I could pursue both sports in the same weekend—or possibly even in the same day?

So during the first week in May, I traveled to South Lake Tahoe to participate in a fund-raising event sponsored by the Heavenly Ski Foundation in support of kids' ski programs. Called "Iced Tee," the event consists of a downhill ski race in the morning, and a golf tournament that same afternoon. Tahoe was the perfect laboratory in which to investigate whether it's worth lugging the gear and dealing with the logistics to move from slopes to slope ratings in such a short period of time. A handful of mountain resorts throughout North America provide the opportunity to pursue this unique biathlon at certain times of year, and some even have ski-golf packages. But should a skiing golfer bother? Early test results suggest one strong conclusion: Anyone conducting similar research should rent something larger than a subcompact automobile, possibly one with four-wheel drive.

En route to Tahoe from the Reno airport to start my grueling adventure, I veered off on a twenty-mile detour to the Dayton Valley Country Club, east of Carson City. In the distance, the snowy spines of the Sierras glinted in bright light, and it thrilled me just a little to think that tomorrow I'd be hammering through mogul fields, even though I was currently on my way to unzip perfect divots out of equally perfect turf. Here in the desert, the temperature was climbing through the seventies, so I donned a pair of khaki shorts and doused myself with sunscreen—an essential item in any ski-golfer's equipage, because mountain sun is deceptively powerful. I tittered with joy and imagined micro-thin briefcase man toughing out a meeting in some stuffy conference room.

As I turned through the front gate, Dayton Valley looked like just another golf course community still waiting for the community, and the Arnold Palmer–designed golf course revealed little of its intrigue. The layout stretched 7,218 yards from the back tees, over rolling hills and gracefully sculpted mounding. The greens tended toward friendly and large. Although the first several holes were fun, they were also forgettable, creating low expectations for any real drama. So when I reached number six—a 163-yard par three with an island green—I was pleasantly surprised. Even more so when I encountered numbers seven through nine, where water squeezed the landing areas, forcing golfers to shape their shots. The last two holes on the front nine presented three lakes—each.

The back side played much the same way, mixing stellar and mundane holes and blending five more lakes into play. The seventeenth, a monstrous par four, measured 478 yards from the back tees. My one frustration with this amicable course was the punitively firm greens, which were more likely to leave a mark on the ball than vice versa.

Yet how could I complain with any real conviction, knowing that I'd have another chance to play golf tomorrow—right after I finished skiing? I drove out of the valley in the late afternoon and began climbing into the mountains. Although I was still dressed for May in the desert, I began to see people emerging from the thickening forests on cross-country skis. The road crested at more than seven thousand feet before dropping down toward the wide blue spill of Lake Tahoe and then bobsledding into town.

The morning of the fund-raiser, I drove to Heavenly Ski Resort's California base lodge for the downhill race. Using some mystical and ancient calculation, organizers of Iced Tee take the top three race times for each team of four participants, convert them into numbers that somehow correspond to a golf score, and add them to the afternoon best-ball results to determine who wins.

Not having ski-raced since I was fourteen, my strategy was simple: Stay alive. It was a good plan, considering that one of the first racers gashed his head open and got carted off to the hospital (*Note:* This did not stop him from playing golf in the afternoon). I managed to get through both my giant slalom runs without falling and before they closed the mountain for the night. I felt better about my slow descent when I learned that the winning time was posted by a former Olympic gold medalist.

Following the ski portion of the event, most of the other participants—who were almost all locals—took off for home, no doubt to squeeze in a power nap, an excellent idea. I spent the rest of the morning exhausting myself by skiing black diamond runs like Waterfall and Ridge Bowl, and riding the nearly empty Sky Express chair to the top of the mountain in seventy-five-degree heat. I skied in jeans, T-shirt, and fleece top, with a Top-Flite golf hat to further aid my transition between sports. At noon, just as the snow melted to slurry, I bounced my way down the mogul-covered East Bowl to my car, where I changed into summer attire, rolled down the windows, and drove up and over a steep pass to reach the Genoa Lakes Golf Club in time for a lunch barbecue.

Designed by Peter Jacobsen, Genoa Lakes plays 7,263 yards from the tips. Although a trophy housing development is beginning to rear its pretentious head, the layout still feels miles from nowhere. The jagged wall of the Sierras fills the view on one side, and the desert valley unfurls toward infinity the other way. When the wind kicks down out of the mountains in the afternoon, golfers will have their hands full even if they didn't ski all morning. If you did, for heaven's sake take a cart.

Playing from the white tees, as we did for the "Tee" part of the Iced Tee, several short par fours offered tantalizing risk-reward ratios. Number three played only 269 yards, but lakes and bunkers gathered overprotectively around the green. The fourth time that one of my well-struck approach shots sailed over the green on the front nine, I realized that altitude is a real factor here. I actually hit one eight-iron 190 yards, causing me to scream, "I da man!"

Despite some heroic shots and clever use of the many mulligans we'd purchased (buy as many as you can: the money goes to charity, and your opponents are sure to maximize their advantages)—and due at least in part to our sluggish performance on the ski slopes—

my team (called Heavenly Overhead) acquired a solid lock on last place in the overall event. If you really want to be competitive, consider finding a friend who happened to win an Olympic medal in skiing, who also has a deadly short game.

On the bright side, I still had another day of skiing and golf ahead of me. I spent the next morning risking my life in Mott Canyon's double-diamond bowls and making twelve runs before lunch. Although I had every intention of playing eighteen holes that afternoon at the Bill Bell–designed Lake Tahoe Golf Course, I went back to my hotel room and slipped into a death sleep instead. The combination of moguls, altitude, and eighty-degree temperatures at the base lodge had really done me in. The biggest danger in trying to maximize ski-golf pleasure is overdoing one to the extent that it impacts your ability to enjoy the other.

My final morning, I skied another dozen runs to close out the season and complete the transition to a full focus on golf. In four days in Tahoe, I'd skied three exhilarating half days, and played thirty-six holes of golf in an alpine funland suspended between winter and spring. Although my experiment suggests that skiing and golfing in the very same day can, in some instances, prove to be too much, next time I'll pace myself, go to sleep earlier, and throttle back my consumption of port.

Some folks might ask why anyone would bother to cram so much activity into such a short time. Some other folks might answer: Because you can. But my question is: Why would you even ask why, unless you have to take your skinny little briefcase into a meeting right about now?

17

Wild A-Bandon

I ONCE WROTE in a magazine that golf courses as good as Oregon's Bandon Dunes come along, oh, about every hundred years or so. Then the Bandon Dunes Resort unveiled its Pacific Dunes golf course. After playing a few early rounds on Pacific Dunes I couldn't help wondering: Had another century flown past so soon?

You cannot talk about Bandon's two supreme layouts without mentioning developer/owner Mike Keiser, a modest, soft-spoken visionary who amassed a fortune in the recycled greeting card business before turning his attention to golf. "I've been to a lot of great golf courses and I'm amazed at how few really sing," Keiser muses. "Most of the truly wonderful courses—outside of Scotland and Ireland—are expensive or inaccessible. But the spirit of golf abides with the public golfer. I wanted to build a great golf course for the avid public golfer that would truly sing."

In fact, the two layouts at Bandon croon, warble, yodel, and chant. They harmonize. They are more boisterous than a passel of Pavarottis belting out an aria that knocks you over backwards in your chair. They keen and wail. But Keiser didn't exactly put this duet of courses together for a song. He spent cash, a lot of it—"A lot more than I originally ever thought I would," he admits. "A lot of people would say, 'What an idiot.' No bank would have loaned even ten percent of the money for this."

In addition to financing the two courses himself—without investors or house lots to sell—Keiser also entrusted the first layout on what may be the most beautiful curl of linksland in America to an architect who had never even designed a golf course on his own before: David MacLay Kidd. Keiser defends this eccentric choice thus: "I admire most name architects but they often superimpose their design style on your site. If you have a great site, why diminish it with a pre-formed sculpture? Finding holes as they were blown in by the wind is a far more poetic use of a great site."

Keiser believed that an unknown architect would more likely allow the golf course to sing in its own voice rather than lip-synching for a famous designer. So for the first layout at Bandon he chose Kidd, whose pedigree included having worked for the Gleneagles Company in Scotland, and having a superintendent father who, according to Keiser, "could make talking about turf grass sound scintillating." For Pacific Dunes, the resort's second layout, Keiser chose Tom Doak, author of two books on course design, architect of a dozen carefully crafted venues, and widely unpopular in the business for his outspoken criticisms of other course designers.

But if Keiser rolled the dice on financing two golf courses in the absolute middle of nowhere, one designed by an architect no one had ever heard of and the other designed by an architect nobody liked, why ruin his streak of strange behavior by actually promoting the place? Bandon Dunes opened in 1999 without huge ceremony or scores of media dignitaries. Management didn't issue press releases or advertise in glossy magazines. Keiser wanted golfers to feel as if they'd discovered Bandon Dunes on their own. Those involved with the project hoped they could put 10,000–12,000 rounds out their first year, and they even wagered on the number. Nobody guessed even close to the 35,000 rounds the course racked up once word spread about this new treasure buried in the sand along the Oregon coast. The opening of Pacific Dunes, while pre-touted in the press and through word-of-mouth, also occured without mountains of hype.

Anyone who's played golf at Bandon knows that something magical and serendipitous is afoot in this location where massive dunes and windblown pines, gorse and fescue roll down to the sea. Originally, Mike Keiser was only able to purchase 1,200 acres of land—adequate for fourteen stellar golf holes and four mediocre ones. But as David Kidd fidgeted with the final routing of the first course, another 400 contiguous acres suddenly went on sale as if through sorcery. The same thing happened when Tom Doak was designing Pacific Dunes and a third parcel of land came on the market, freeing him to whip up a truly exceptional layout. If good fortune is a measure of mysterious forces working in your favor, Mike Keiser is clearly the Roy Hobbs (Robert Redford's role in *The Natural*) of golf course development. He is some kind of genius. And he is another rare thing: a man with vision and the money to realize it, but also a man who cares about doing things right.

Visitors who've experienced Pac Dunes whisper about the new course with a reverence usually reserved for mistresses or first cars. Status among west coast golfers is now bestowed based upon how early you managed to play at this new and future windswept Mecca of American golf.

Although the new course resides along a stunning piece of rugged northwest coastline adjacent to the site of the original Bandon Dunes course, it is entirely different not only in architectural style but in topography. Seven holes play along the ocean, but the inland holes journey in and around humongous dunes scantily clad in gorse and beach grasses. These holes are insular—not only wind-protected but somehow hobbitlike. Dunes define this course the way they define Pete Dye's work at Whistling Straits (in fact, Doak— along with extraordinarily talented shaper Jim Urbina—trained under Dye). But Bandon's dunes weren't trucked in from Idaho. They've lain here beneath the wind and storms and eagle turds (and bear scat!) for centuries.

If the original Bandon Dunes golf course keens the woof and whorl of a true Scottish links, if it appears glazed with single malt and orates like Sean Connery, tastes like shortbread and grilled lamb and sounds plaintive and lovely and moving as bagpipes at sunset, then the new Pacific Dunes is its Irish cousin: deep and rich as the perfect pint of Guinness, sweet as Irish cream, lively as a fiddle jig played in the back room of a warm tavern on a night when chill winds tear across the moors. It wafts flavorful hints of Ballybunion, Lahinch and Royal County Down.

Whereas Bandon Dunes greets with a wide, welcoming embrace of golf that rolls like foam-edged ocean waves, Pacific Dunes tunnels between huge sand blowouts, insular, secret, impish. Shore pines gather and scatter like elegant spectators wearing funny, windblown green hats. Leprechauns surely lurk beneath the sharp and yellow gorse mounds and whisper with reverence the words: Tom. Doak. Doak and Urbina didn't push dirt around the site so much as they spooned it, allowing every lovely natural undulation to express itself like a gentle sonnet. Of the land Doak says simply, "You work your whole life to get a piece of property this good."

Pac Dunes is a lot shorter than Bandon Dunes; though the par-71 layout can stretch to 6,827 yards from the longest of three sets of tees, it will be set up to play around 6,300 yards for most sensible golfers. The greens are smaller than those of its older neighbor, but the new course can roar like a battle hymn, especially when the wind howls along. It is nothing if not epic, and you'd be hard pressed to find its equal anywhere outside the British Isles.

Pacific Dunes opens amidst pines and dramatic inland dunes and moundings. The sinuous first fairway rises in cresting green humps and then folds down toward a flattish green tucked into a dune that flows both toward it and away like a lava dome. Movements throughout the course are liquid—alternately as sweeping and force-ful as whitewater and as slow as tapioca.

On the first two holes, positioning on the left side of the fairway allows for views of the greens, which should remind golfers that accurate positioning will remain important throughout their round. By the third hole, the topography spills wide to reveal a sylvan val-ley islanded with bunkers floating in the emerald rivers of fairway that flow alongside, away from, and down toward the sea.

Number four, the first oceanside gift, frolics for 460 yards along cliffs a hundred feet above crashing surf to a green that totters on the precipice as if one more golf ball might tumble the whole thing to the beach below. The 316-yard sixth is a "mini-me" of Pac Dunes' character: the fairway licks between high mounds to a narrow, ele-vated green that drops steeply on both sides. The dune/bunker complex supporting the left side seems to whisper disparaging remarks about your backswing. To reach the garden spot, smack a slight fade over a right-side fairway bunker to a place you can't know even has grass until you've played the hole before. Coming in from this position vaccinates you against the dune and affords a direct line at the green.

Even ordinary holes such as 405-yard number seven crackle with evocative touches—here, weird natural moundings fifty yards out impart a hummocky British picnic feel. The ninth hole, one of the most Irish, calls for a drive up and over a huge ridge of dunes to a blind fairway, and presents one of the few risk/reward options on the course: how much sand to chew off. The miles-wide fairway plays to one of two alternating greens either above or below.

The back nine begins with two oceanside par threes—205 yards threaded downhill right at the ocean, then 145 yards along seaside bluffs to a green camoflauged in dun-colored grasses. When you've finished with number eleven, you'll be searching for Tom Doak to give him a hug. How could anyone not like a guy who designs golf courses this good?

Number thirteen may be Pac Dunes' best hole. Tee off across cliffs at a humongous dune planet to a fairway that seems to share DNA with the best holes at Spanish Bay. The duneside green lies 440 treacherous yards from the tee. Tunnels and secret passageways head inland through the dunes just as you'll do on the 345-yard risk/reward sixteenth hole, where green moguls roll like some fantastically skewed ski run. The finishing hole, which can play as long as 660 yards, is a puzzlement of angles and prodigious bunkers defending both fairway and green.

Pacific Dunes has already joined hands with Bandon Dunes near the top of most experts' lists of best courses—it is that good. The Resort should give Pebble Beach a run for its money, especially as Bandon is half the price.

As Pac Dunes finishes greening beneath the Oregon spring in anticipation of another summer, folks are wondering about a rumored third course. All Mike Keiser will say is that if it does occur, he'll hire a different architect to build a wind-protected woodlands venue that will sing a very different if equally catchy tune. I'll await the encore with great impatience. In the meantime, I'll play the existing courses and sleep in the resort's small hotel at night only because you can't really play golf in the dark. As if I could sleep. As if anyone could, knowing what's out there.

18

The Wild and Ancient

LET'S SAY THAT you snap-hook your approach shot on the thir-teenth hole of the Moab Golf Club, in southeastern Utah, into the startling redrock desert surrounding the course. It's early morning, and the fairways are deserted except for jackrabbits, so you climb the wooden border fence and walk toward a wall of slick, polished sand-stone to look for your ball. You carry a nine-iron as much to defend against rattlesnakes as to use for your next shot. A moment later, as you bend over to pluck your wayward Titleist out of the sagebrush, you're suddenly aware of being watched. You look up: face to face with Moab Man, a seven-hundred-year-old petroglyph pecked into the rock face by an ancient Anasazi Indian.

The artwork is frightening in a primitive and yet somehow vaguely familiar way, all passion and rough technique. It depicts a wild anthromorph wearing what might be basketball-sized earrings, and sporting antlers, and waving his arms in a pose that suggests either worship or warning. If Moab Man were alive, you'd surely offer to let him play through.

The Four Corners region—where the states of Utah, Colorado, Arizona, and New Mexico abut—encompasses high mesas and deep, stream-carved canyons and lonely expanses of sand and stone awash in such archaeological postcards sent by the Anasazi. This extinct tribe of Native Americans built intricate cliff dwellings here amid some of the most rugged and spectacular topography in the world. They engineered and constructed beautiful multistory buildings, created perfectly round underground ceremonial chambers (called kivas), built dams and irrigation systems, and drew galleries of rock art, all without the use of anything but stone tools. Many of these sites—which have survived thanks to a dry climate and protected locations—look just as they must have when the Anasazi inexplicably abandoned their homeland and disappeared into history seven centuries ago.

Archaeologists offer a number of possible explanations as to why the Anasazi departed, including drought, overpopulation, resource depletion, hostile neighbors, and the lure of the Kachina religion farther to the south. Most agree that the Anasazi are probably ancestors of such modern pueblo tribes as the Hopi and Acoma. But as Fred Sherman, a park ranger and guide at Navajo National Monument in Arizona told me while we explored the ghostly ruins of Keet Seel, sometimes science doesn't provide the most important parts of what's true.

Whatever you choose to believe about their disappearance, there is a palpable eeriness to the Anasazi legacy. These were not knuckle-dragging savages, but modern people who developed art and technology, loved each other, felt regret and experienced joy just like us, but who for some reason failed to survive. Lacking a formal written language, they never recorded their history, so all that we really know of their culture is implied by stone ruins and strange rock art. Today these sites are moving in a way that we cannot understand rationally—which is part of their powerful attraction.

Possibly we are drawn to such remote signs of the Anasazi because they put us in direct touch with what Jung referred to as "the collective unconscious"—what we inexplicably remember from a much earlier time in history. Standing among the stone ruins of the once-lovely village at Keet Seel, gazing down at the stream that winds through the canyon, tasting the flavor of cliffrose on the breeze, we're touched by nostalgia. We pine for forgotten places that we can't even say we've ever been.

Folks who are drawn to such cryptic messages from the past, for whatever reasons, can discover thousands of unmarked Anasazi sites just by knowing what to look for on hikes and backpack trips throughout the mesas and canyons of the Southwest. The best way to encounter the ruins, and to engage their mysteries, is in the backcountry, without maps (except topographical maps), tour guides, fences, or, in many cases, even trails. In a book titled *Abstract Wild,* the writer Jack Abbott suggests that archaeological sites retain a certain aura of sacredness in the wilderness that they lack in parks, where every visitor robs another tiny amp of their power. Suddenly looking skyward from a canyon floor and spotting the black squares of windows high up in some stream-carved alcove, or unexpectedly coming upon the red-painted palm prints of an ancient family pressed onto the rock wall above their former home, purveys the kind of excitement you might feel upon reuniting with someone you loved once but lost contact with long ago.

For those with less time or little inclination to sleep out in the wilderness, more accessible ruins (and some of the most impressive) can be seen at national parks and monuments such as Keet Seel, Chaco Canyon, Mesa Verde, and Hovenweep. Wherever you encounter remnants of the Anasazi, remember to tread carefully in the ruins and leave all artifacts where you find them—for the sake of both posterity and your own peace of mind. At least one backcountry ranger I know attests to receiving pot shards and other artifacts in the mail nearly every day from people who took them home from archaeological sites and inexplicably suffered all varieties of misfortune.

While driving between sites you can stop at a handful of excellent, underplayed golf venues (and a couple of really scrubby ones) and contemplate the unarticulatable mysteries of that primitive game, pursuing further connections between the ancient and modern. Also meditate upon the irony that Anasazi civilization may have collapsed because they couldn't water their food crops in a land where we currently irrigate fairways full of green, useless grass.

In the same way that more remote archaeological sites exude the most power, the wildest golf courses—overgrown with native fescues, buffeted by cold sea winds, carved through ancient forests, requiring daunting carries over rivers or arroyos—often provide the most profound golf experiences. We seek out dramatic venues because they put us in touch with at least a remnant of what is organic and untamed. For many folks who've settled into sedentary lives, the golf course may be as close to wildness as they're likely to get.

Standing on the thirteenth fairway of the Moab Golf Club, for example, or on the windblown ninth at Turnberry's Ailsa Course, or at any number of wildly natural golf courses framed by deserts or rain forests, we may also recall some distant memory of the game in its purest form. The instinct that compels some folks to search for old Indian ruins drives others to travel the world playing the same game over and over in different locales: a desire to explore something external that ultimately leads us back to ourselves.

As ranger Fred Sherman told me at Keet Seel, archaeologists and scientists and historians (including golf historians) only have facts. Ultimately, more meaningful answers come to us from our collective unconscious, as we gaze at ruins across some desolate canyon or watch clouds gather and disperse above a distant green and we feel the dry wind, and long for a life—pure and unmanicured—that something inside us remembers with a lonesome ache.

For a downright strange juxtaposition, consider alternating visits to Anasazi sites and out-of-the-way golf courses throughout the Southwest. Following are only some of the more obvious, mostly frontcountry destinations; the real fun is in devising a more personal journey that invites the unexpected.

CHACO CULTURE NATIONAL HISTORIC PARK, NAGEEZI, NEW MEXICO

Consider the words of another park ranger: G. B. Cornucopia, a white-bearded philosopher who's spent years among the so-called great house ruins at Chaco Canyon, in northwestern New Mexico. Standing before Hungo Pavi—a tumble of still-crisp masonry walls, roofless kivas, and open plazas—Cornucopia addressed the ancient mysteries that cluster around the ruins like tumbleweed. "The longer I'm here, the more mysterious this all becomes," he said. "Every question has three or four answers. It's all guesswork. If you look for hard-and-fast answers, you'll be frustrated, but if you can ask open-ended questions, you'll be fascinated." Ranger Cornucopia could just as well have offered this as a Zen-like lesson at any number of alternative golf schools.

In fact, much about Chaco Canyon defies rational explanation. Archaeologists estimate that early residents carried nearly a quarter of a million trees from as far away as sixty miles to build the great houses here. For approximately four centuries, this sprawling site stood at the center of the Anasazi empire both geographically and in terms of its influence. An extensive system of ancient roads thirty feet wide and stretching for four hundred miles connected Chaco with seventy-five other ancient towns, suggesting that many people came to visit during the Anasazi era. Still, the lack of hearths, trash mounds, and burials implies that few resided here. Because many of the numerous structures were not regularly inhabited, some researchers have posited that Chaco served as a trading post; yet even though excavations have revealed hundreds of thousands of pots, hundreds of turquoise pendants, innumerable beads, and even such rarities as copper bells, seashells, and macaw feathers, there's little evidence that the Chacoans ever created anything that left the site. To add to the layers of mystery, world-renowned photographer William Jackson shot more than four hundred photos of Chaco in 1870. None came out.

As a hot wind blew through Hungo Pavi during my visit, ranger Cornucopia posited that perhaps Chaco Canyon was a sort of pilgrimage site seven hundred years ago—a powerful place that the Anasazi visited to get in touch with something that was elusive in their everyday lives, a kind of primitive's St. Andrews. Following a pause filled only with the sound of ravens calling, the ranger asked if that isn't exactly how we use the place today. "We are the Chacoans now," he remarked.

PINON HILLS GOLF COURSE, FARMINGTON, NEW MEXICO

The moon would be as likely a location for this artful Ken Dye golf course on the far edge of the middle of nowhere. *Golf Digest* rates Pinon Hills as one of eight five-star public courses in the nation. It isn't quite that good until you consider the green fees; Pinon Hills may be the best golf value not located in the third world.

While masochists can play the 7,249-yard gold tees (with a 140 slope), the whites, at 6,239/128, still offer plenty of challenge. Nearly every tee shot requires some carry over arroyos or desert, and a number of holes on the back side play across and even down into lovely slickrock canyons. The terrain rolls through cedar, piñon, and juniper trees with occasional views of distant white mesas that are probably littered with ancient ruins. Fairways are luxurious, and the greens are mostly large, three-tiered, and fun. Aesthetic bunkering adds to the crisp design. The fifteenth, a 173-yard par three, is Pinon Hills' signature hole; it features nine tee box locations in and around a canyon, and incorporates a sand arroyo from tee to green, grassy humps, and white slickrock, with a few cliffs and boulders thrown in. Pinon Hills finishes with two par fives; the eighteenth requires strategic shotmaking between two arroyos, and suffers no shortage of sand.

NAVAJO NATIONAL MONUMENT, KAYENTA, ARIZONA

After hiking eight and a half miles across a mesa and down through northeastern Arizona's Tsegi Canyon—filled with box elder, aspen, oak, and fir—your eyes will suddenly be drawn to stripes of blood-red desert varnish staining the roof of a vast alcove, and pointing down at the ruin called Keet Seel. The ancient village hangs like an elevated green on a shelf behind a retaining wall that stretches 180 feet across the eastern half of the alcove. The ends of long wooden poles protrude from the wall: Bent slightly inward under the weight of backfill, these logs have pulled the wall away from the edge for centuries, a brilliant piece of engineering.

As you approach the site, thousands of colorful pot shards bearing intricate patterns lie revealed in the ancient dust. The ruin itself—accessible by climbing a series of ladders—hosts a scattering of more shards, stone tools, corncobs, turkey feathers, and a wealth of other artifacts. Up in the alcove, beautiful square buildings with sleek lines are arranged along three main streets. The rooms and kivas display various designs, suggesting that many different people influenced the architecture.

The first village was built at Keet Seel in A.D. 950. In 1250 another town was constructed atop the first. According to tree-ring dating, 1272 was a particularly busy year for building, but by 1300 all of the residents had fled. Before leaving forever, the Anasazi inhabitants sealed their doorways with large, fitted stones, possibly because they expected to return. Approximately 125 people lived here, but curiously, only eleven burials were ever found.

Questions, contradictions, and mysteries abound. Our Native guide, Fred Sherman, told us that many of his people believe the ruins are haunted. Several Navajo rangers have reported getting flustered, tongue-tied, strangely fatigued, and otherwise self-conscious while giving tours of the site. A number of modern tribes, including the Navajos, recognize aspects of their own rituals in the clues the Anasazi left behind. Sherman admitted that some of the rock art executed in these canyons depicts clan symbols still familiar to his people today.

Later that evening, I spoke with Sherman across a small fire of piñon and juniper at my campsite. A half-moon spotlit the ruins, and the dark squares of the doorways seemed like portals to another time. Listening to his stories, I wondered how much the ranger knew that he wasn't telling, and whether his people are still intrinsically linked to something that most of us have lost our connection to.

MOAB GOLF CLUB, MOAB, UTAH

Set between rolling slickrock dunes and a sheer-walled red mesa, Moab's lush green fairways create a stunning counterpoint. Although holes are neatly grassed and groomed, the surrounding topography creates a wild feel. This rock-solid layout is perfect for contemplating the way passing clouds absorb color and spread it across the sky.

Designed by a group of locals, the course stretches to 6,819 yards (and a 125 slope) from the back tees, which mostly add only modest distance, and not another degree of difficulty. A scattering of elevated tees and greens offer glimpses of the La Sal Mountains, and cottonwoods edging several fairways provide welcome shade. A handful of holes practically play up into the slickrock desert. Moab's best hole is number five, a 455-yard par five that drops down from an elevated tee before tempting you to launch a heroic approach across narrowing fairway to an elevated amphitheater green. The course includes a few farmland holes, but all the views are keepers. You'll encounter everyone from Mormon insurance salesmen to ragged mountain bikers, and if you wander into the ever-encroaching desert, you'll surely turn up signs of the Anasazi as well.

MESA VERDE NATIONAL PARK, BETWEEN CORTEZ AND MANCOS, COLORADO

Imagine that it's December 1888, and you're rounding up stray cows in a snowstorm in southwestern Colorado with your brother-in-law. Looking down into a steep canyon from the rim, squinting into the snow for lonely heifers, you suddenly make out the edges of a huge stone edifice that later proves to be the largest cliff dwelling ever discovered in North America: Cliff Palace, consisting of 217 rooms, twenty-three kivas, and round and square towers spread across six levels in a huge white sandstone alcove high above the canyon floor.

The Weatherill family—cowboys and amateur archaeologists who discovered Cliff Palace and excavated many of the most impressive ruins in the Southwest—would be dismayed to visit the site where it now lies within Mesa Verde National Park. Sadly, our modern attraction to such powerful pilgrimage sites has led to the over-management and commercialization of the most dramatic Anasazi ruins. Many—like Cliff Palace—have been transformed into parodies of sacredness, a sort of Church of Elvis that provides only the most tenuous connection to what can so deeply move us upon discovering such locales.

At Mesa Verde, visitors will experience the worst of what the curmudgeonly western writer Ed Abbey called "industrial tourism." Mesa Verde is currently as mild and tricked up as a putt-putt course, replete with huge gift shops and cornball tours requiring advance ticket purchases. The park is so commercialized that while driving the loop road you'll encounter a billboard for an Indian casino. The place lacks only a windmill and a giant plaster bunny.

On my ranger-led excursion to the remarkable Cliff Palace, I considered hiding in one of the ancient structures until all the ice-cream-licking, ALL I GOT WAS THIS LOUSY T-SHIRT–wearing visitors had left, and the rangers had locked the gates behind them for the night. I hungered for a moment of repose in the ruins—the same desire that led me to walk the Old Course at St. Andrews after midnight to connect with its wild spirit free of golfers elbowing each other to shoot photos on the Swilcan Bridge. The closest I came at Mesa Verde was on a private tour of Spruce Tree House, when my guide encouraged me to carefully stick my head through a window and breathe the same air that the Anasazi once breathed. Inside the structure, a painting of red mountain peaks on the plastered wall, and the cool scent of juniper cheered me the same way it must have given pleasure to the inhabitants of a previous millennium.

DALTON RANCH AND GOLF CLUB, DURANGO, COLORADO

Ken Dye's "American links configuration" at Dalton Ranch runs alongside the muddy Animas River in the lee of the San Juan Mountains. The course plays from 5,539 to 6,934 yards with a maximum slope of 125. Load up on cool mountain winds, commune with pine and aspen, and prepare to have your hands full with the large, tiery greens.

River, streams, OB, and some misanthropically untamed grasses suggest that the sensible approach on several holes is to leave your driver back in your kiva. On 378-yard number six, lay up for a second shot over a rocky waterfall and notice how the curvaceous moundings reflect distant hills. Number ten also calls for discipline: Water crosses the fairway 240 yards out, so hit six-iron/eight-iron on this lively 315-yard tease. Complete your day by hitting to an eighteenth green that practically floats in the river. On the far shore, an old homestead will remind you of the region's more recent though less civilized western legacy.

HOVENWEEP NATIONAL MONUMENT, BETWEEN BLANDING, UTAH, AND CORTEZ, COLORADO

At dusk, the remote ruins of Hovenweep's Square Tower site soak up the red color of the sunset and cast angling shadows across the rim of the mesa. Nine surviving structures cluster together as if for companionship along the rim and in the bottom of a whiterock canyon that would make for a challenging carry. The sloping sides of the canyon are filled with rubble from other collapsed buildings that might have enclosed a plaza and created an insular community feeling here seven centuries ago.

The most imposing of the remaining structures is Hovenweep Castle, a multistory ruin with a sheer wall built to the edge of the mesa and a window directly overlooking the chasm, suggesting that in addition to functional concerns, the Anasazi appreciated a dramatic view. At the northwest end of the castle, a D-shaped tower contains small portals that still cast sunlight upon interior architectural details on the days of solstices and equinoxes. Below the castle, Square Tower itself rises tipsily from its foundation atop a large, irregular boulder.

Hovenweep's towers are the most puzzling aspect of the six sites spread throughout the monument. Archaeologists guess that these unusual structures may have been defensive in nature, or perhaps served as ceremonial chambers, food storage areas, communications posts, or celestial observatories. Which is to say, they don't really know.

The Anasazi first began farming in the area two thousand years ago, and erected their villages along Hovenweep's canyons by A.D. 1200. A century later, the estimated twenty-five hundred inhabitants were gone. Researchers guess that the Square Tower neighborhood itself housed about a hundred people in two hundred rooms. Residents would have spent their days hunting, farming, construct-ing buildings, making ceramics and jewelry, and perhaps visiting neighbors and family members in the evenings as the air grew cool and drew them toward moments of repose.

But science cannot tell us what the residents felt like leaving this lovely canyon system, abandoning a society they'd struggled to cre-ate in the desert. Did the most intuitive among them suspect that the very existence of their culture perched on the edge of a precipice, and was about to plunge over? And was the view anything like the way our own society looks to us today?

Sadness and the scent of blooming cliffrose perfume the air at Hovenweep. Prickly pear cactus and orange globe mallow push up through the ruins, toppling them back into the desert, growing over what's left of our connection to those who came before us here.

THE CLIFFS GOLF COURSE AT TAMARRON HILTON RESORT, DURANGO, COLORADO

Golfers suffering from acrophobia should avoid The Cliffs, an inspiring collection of rugged mountaineer's golf holes designed— appropriately enough—by Arthur Hills. The Cliffs plays 6,885/142 from the Kahuna tees and 6,340/135 for mere mortals, but remember that you're at sevety-six hundred feet of elevation: high enough for your normal club selections to sail sleeves of balls over the tricky greens. Bluegrass fairways, wildflowers, and views of the San Juan Mountains will tempt you to pick your head up on every swing. Several holes showcase pine and aspen groves climbing steep rocky slopes, and a hundred shades of green reflect light in the sweet alpine air.

The most dramatic holes build to a climactic finish, starting with number fourteen, where a resident comedian lives under a rock—hence the local rule that reads, "Automatic free drop in cases of ball theft by yellow-bellied marmots." Holes fifteen through eighteen all bring blue mountain lakes into play, and water threatens on twelve holes overall. The greens, which just plain slope rather than undulating, are deadly. The best—and most controversial—hole is the sixteenth, a 415-yard hairpin turn that drops faster than an overweight rappeller, over a cliff toward a green surrounded by meadowy lakes. The Anasazi would have felt right at home on this golf course.

PART THREE

*Eccentric
Personalities*

19

Men in Green

IN A MEETING room at the Bandon Dunes Resort on the southern Oregon coast, approximately two dozen men are planning to
make you mad—if not today, then soon. Not necessarily on purpose,
but it seems inevitable. They're not evil or mean-spirited, these men
with names like Jim and Josh and even Robin and Dana. They love
their families. They enjoy good beer. Some wear goofy shoes, others
are hip and sport shapely goatees. Individually they are funny, sullen,
driven, artistic, impatient, dry-humored, argumentative, outspoken,
and even cuddly. As a whole they are a bunch of brainiacs. They work
hard for little recognition in places like China and New Zealand and
North Dakota, in the wind, rain, hail, dust, and heat.

One of them once lost the only golf ball in the entire country
of Latvia. Another spent three million dollars constructing a single
par-three hole in Guam, where storms destroyed several rounds of
work and relocated cart paths into the trees (and nearly carried the
superintendent out to sea).

You don't know these men, but they talk about you all the
time—and not always fondly (in a moment of frustration, one of
them says that 80 percent of you suck). They can influence your

mood and ruin your mojo and chances are you'll spend some summer days in their company sometime soon without even knowing it. They may consider whether you say "golf course" or "goff course" as a fashion statement.

Surely you've guessed that they are young (mostly), as-yet-unheralded golf course architects—not the famous ones whose names you'd know even if you didn't play golf. These are the supporting casts, the guys who will frustrate you more a year from now, or five years, when the trajectories of their bright stars rise and flash across the sky. The ones who worked (or still work) for other men who get the credit for their efforts because life is not fair. Although those gathered here count several dozen of America's best-ranked modern courses among their credentials, many labor unnoticed in New England or Canada, or they toil in the strange far corners of the third world, or they only perform renovations.

They have come together at Bandon Dunes at the behest of one who might be the most talented little-known course designer in the business: Tom Doak, of Renaissance Golf Design. Doak is an architect's architect: He believes in classical elements of style, he's not shy about lambasting bad design work, and he's written two books on golf architecture that have become cult classics. Doak recently finished Pacific Dunes, the new course that will open at Bandon Dunes in July. In honor of his fortieth birthday, and to show off his latest creation, Doak organized this summit, which participants are calling Archipalooza. They have ventured here to talk business and get to know each other.

If you think that golf course designers sit around discussing bunkers and turf grass, you're partly right. They also talk about "Jack" and "Pete" and "Bobby," mostly with respect, but not always nicely. They commiserate over how much they hate trees.

Over this long weekend they also hold actual meetings, the minutes of which might read something like this:

Ate breakfast.

Discussed hot topics:

1. Course rankings: Are they a positive thing?

2. Liability, especially as relates to cart paths.

3. "Fast and firm": an issue or a style?

Adjourned for golf.

Later, they present slide shows and share their opinions and experiences and humorous war stories. Tom Doak recalls how a friend once claimed that he never hit into Doak's bunkers, so Doak began tucking bunkers closer to his greens. There's a lesson here: Be careful what you tell golf course architects.

If it weren't for these men (the only women in sight all weekend are waitresses), every modern track would be designed in the style of Robert Trent Jones. Which is why, when you enjoy golf courses, you should take note of who designed them and remember architects' names.

On a certain Sunday when you play well and meet the challenges of a skillfully crafted layout, you will thank these men. You will admire and respect them. You will curse them.

They will smile in response, knowing they've succeeded at their difficult work.

20

Family Affair

I'VE ALWAYS BEEN fond of both adventure travel and golf, and I recently had the opportunity to combine the two—by undertaking an adventurous golf trip with my girlfriend Reneé and my parents. What could be more fraught with danger than risking twelve hours in the car with Mom and Dad?

It happened like this: Reneé and I decided to spend last Thanksgiving with my folks in Florida. To help defer trip costs, I landed an assignment to visit and write about the new Ocean Hammock Golf Club, in Palm Coast. The course was so new management assured me I'd be the first person to ever play the spacious Jack Nicklaus oceanside design, which would open officially two weeks after my visit. Not even Jack had golfed the completed layout. I smelled course record!

It also happens that my father has played golf nearly his entire life; it's his most intense passion. When I was growing up, the game provided his sole diversion from a six-day work week. It's also one of few interests we share. I figured taking my dad along to Ocean Hammock might give him a small thrill. For the past several months, he'd been recovering from cancer surgery that involved removing part of his hipbone, and he'd been making slow progress. Mom reported that even after a few weeks, he could barely maneuver his walker to the front yard, where he likes to hold court in his bathrobe, smoking and greeting the neighbors.

Before the surgery (his third in recent years), Dad's doctor promised him he'd eventually be able to play golf again. I suspected that golf was driving his recovery. Each Sunday when we spoke on the phone, he'd boast about the five ghost swings he'd executed in the living room, or tell me that he'd picked up and gripped an actual club. I hoped that setting a deadline by which he would need to actually hit full shots might speed his convalescence. If he wasn't up to it, I told him, I'd hit all the long shots and he could chip and putt—a sort of modified father-son scramble.

In putting together this golf game, and inviting Mom and Reneé along, I had an ulterior motive, as well: to draw my parents and my girlfriend together in a way that might bond them. Although Mom has never even ventured a practice swing, I figured she could drive one of the carts, and maybe provide some color commentary if anyone happened to hit a good shot.

When I first pitched this particular story to my editor at *Links* magazine, he feared a syrupy, overdramatic tale of love and reconciliation with altogether too much potential for hugging. He suggested that everything didn't necessarily have to work out smoothly. I knew he was rooting for at least a minor blow-up, if not a full-on festival of family dysfunction.

Which I thought about during the six-hour drive from Delray Beach to Palm Coast, as my dad read aloud every road sign we flew past.

"Look, honey. Stuckeys," he said thirty-two times.

"Look, honey. Dollar ninety-nine super value meal," he repeated every twelve miles.

For her part, after asking several times when and where we wanted to eat, Mom forced us to have lunch at the Cracker Barrel "no earlier than twelve-thirty" but, it turned out, no later than twelve-thirty, either.

The stellar staff at Ocean Hammock Golf Club currently top my list of people whom I wish lottery jackpots upon, and they are all welcome at my own door at any time. Under the sensitive oversight of head pro Chuck Kandt, they treated us like visiting dignitaries despite the pressure of having to open a new golf course in two weeks. They welcomed us with sparkling rental clubs, sleeves of balls, logoed shirts, boxed lunches, and that rarest of all things at golf courses today: genuine hospitality. I believed they were actually glad to see us. My parents—who'd not really witnessed me "at work" before—were impressed.

Following our warm reception, two O.H. staff members escorted us to the practice range, where four perfect pyramids of golf balls glistened on the untouched grass. Twenty minutes later we all stood nervously on the number one tee as the marshal finished his orientation and invited us to let fly the first official shots on this virgin course. I stepped up and absolutely *ripped* a high fade far down the center of the fairway. Reneé, who only golfs occasionally, and only occasionally well, unwrapped her long, lovely, and often dazzlingly inaccurate swing to punch a respectable line drive out into the green expanse.

I'd played enough golf with my dad to know that he would swing hard and clumsily, stepping away from the ball at the same time that he tried to kill it dead, and thereby stub an embarrassing dribbler to the end of the tee box. I held another ball in my pocket, ready to proffer the requisite mulligan.

But Dad teed off with a three-iron and modeled the best swing I'd seen him make in two decades, following through to a perfect finish position and only looking up in time to see the result land and bounce in the center of the fairway 160 yards out. Mom smiled, no doubt assuming he always executed shots like this.

Out on the fairway, Dad nutted another long iron to just short of the elevated green, pitched close to the pin, and made the first par ever recorded on Ocean Hammock. He hadn't performed this well since the Carter administration. After being unable to get out on the course for so long, Dad had come to play.

We went on in this way, hitting some fine shots and a few not worth describing. After several frustrating holes swinging her ladies' rental set, Reneé switched to my clubs and suddenly adopted a new golf personality. She tied my bogey four on the 146-yard fourth hole, which amused her to no end. We laughed a lot, and nearly melted into a group hug several times. Who knew that hanging with loved ones could be this much fun?

Not to disappoint my editor, there was tension, too. I spent much of the day managing these golfers who lost themselves in the scenery, in the wonder of balls and grass and palms dancing in the wind; at one point a foursome of tortoises asked if they could maybe play through. Additionally, I had to explain the ninety-degree cart rule to my dad at least one time for each degree. And throughout the round, he continually exclaimed "Nice shot!" even when I sliced a drive into the tullies, topped an approach into a bunker, or bladed a chip over the green. He wanted them to be nice shots; what could I say? Reneé, on the other hand, couldn't seem to remember that the higher the number on the club, the shorter the distance it hit the ball. Mom, for her part, at first refused to drive the cart altogether; when she relented, she still wouldn't take it out onto the fairways, which was necessary to minimize Dad's walk to his ball. Mom was also skeptical of that ninety-degree thing.

On the seventh hole, a reef of thunderclouds gathered offshore, threatening a storm of biblical proportions. Lightning cleaved the sky, sliding closer all the time. I willed it away, prayed that the weather would not ruin this rare opportunity. But on the eighth hole, where the gray ocean suddenly popped into view as we walked up to the green, the marshal asked us to come inside. It rained like it only can in the Tropics—hard enough to drive nails—as we ate lunch huddled in the makeshift clubhouse. Then, twenty minutes later, the sky lightened; we'd been granted a reprieve.

On the back nine, I recognized that we were in a race to finish before dark and I herded my family along like a sheepdog nipping at the animals to keep them moving when they wished only to graze. On the last two holes, as we squinted to see our drives against the darkening sky, I thought: *We'll never make it. My family won't simultaneously hold the men's, women's, and senior course records, if only for a day.*

But somehow we chipped up to the eighteenth green as night-fall slurped the final light off the ocean. Back at the clubhouse, the staff greeted us like Odysseus returned home after his long journey.

We scored no holes-in-one that day. We staged no dramatic scenes of connection or reconciliation—but there were no shouting match-es either. We exhibited no kissy-faced earnestness. We played golf steadily and sometimes quietly and occasionally well. We switched cart partners every six holes so everyone had a chance to ride with everyone else. We were simply a family playing golf in the afternoon, hoping to finish before the rains came again or darkness fell.

My dad shot 103 with the help of some slightly creative score-keeping. Who's really to say that a seventy-five-year-old man recovering from surgery and playing his first full round of golf in months shouldn't be allowed to retee whenever he damned well feels like it? Which is why I advocate an amendment to the rules of golf: a mulligan for every radiation treatment undergone with quiet dignity. A conceded putt for each painful step from walker to walking again.

After our round, Dad admitted that in half a century of golfing, this was the best experience he'd ever enjoyed. He talks about it still.

For me it was equally as good. For an entire afternoon of sun-breaks and thunderstorms, swaying palms and sunken putts, I trav-eled through a beautiful place with only my parents and the woman I love. We created some stories that we'll continue to tell for years to come. And I watched my aging father unobtrusively, and without comment or complaint, set the Ocean Hammock senior course record and simultaneously kick cancer's ass. I have never been more proud.

21

Robert Trent Jones Jr. and the Edges of Doom

TALKING WITH THE most famous son of the most famous father of modern golf course architecture, it's hard to tell this junior Jones from his fictitious namesake, Indiana. Bobby—as Robert Trent Jones Jr. prefers to be called—has made a life in golf into the kind of adventurous exploration that's become rare on our increasingly developed planet. As he says, "I'll go to the ends of the earth just so you'll follow."

Behind many of his more than two hundred golf designs in dozens of states and thirty-eight foreign countries on six continents stands a man who works on many levels, who welcomes a new challenge, and who sees the game and his pursuit of it as not just a physical—but as a metaphysical—journey.

Like the best writers and artists, Jones employs subtext and symbolism, imagery and illusion, as well as a range of other techniques from the verbal and visual arts to express aspects of philosophy, drama, and aesthetics. And his courses tell stories.

Jones may actually be an even better storyteller than he is a designer. Ask him a question and he'll string together anecdotes and adventure tales from his travels around the globe, dropping the names of famous golfers, celebrities, and political figures. Yet while he enjoys being the center of attention—whether at a cocktail party hosted by U.S. Ambassador to Barbados Hyde, or drinking a beer in the clubhouse after a round of golf—Jones is also eager, interested, and absorbed in what other people have to say. He is generous, genuine, and thoroughly likable, if also impatient and strong-willed. He also possesses an admirable short game.

I spent a long weekend with Jones as he put the finishing touches on the back nine of his new Royal Westmoreland Golf Course in Barbados. Our interviews took place at crowded lunch tables, over rum punches on the beach, at dinner parties, and out on the golf course. Playing with Jones provides a view of golf course design the depths of which most people would never fathom. Talking with him provides an opportunity to discuss aspects of the game that don't receive nearly enough attention in conversation or in print.

One lasting impression: After hitting a mediocre approach shot on the dramatic quarry hole (number six) at Royal Westmoreland, Jones faced an impossible sidehill putt on a slick, sloping green. After studying it from various angles and frowning his displeasure, he looked up from his ball and said: "I designed it, so I'll have to play it."

Did you learn anything in particular at Yale that has helped in your career?

RTJ Jr.: I learned how to think. During the time I was there, Yale offered a very strict education. I studied geology, which was useful later on. As an American studies and history major (liberal arts), I learned to write and to pursue highly critical thinking. And I learned how to learn—how to go to a source like the library, or an older person, and learn what I needed to know from that source, and apply my own thinking to it.

My education has helped me read golf history with a different eye. I might read about a course in India and wonder what the British were doing there, and why. I learned how to ask a historian's questions: What motivated them to bring their game there and put it inside a horse paddock? Why were there walls around those places? What was going on? By asking these questions you see how the golf courses themselves were interpreted through the environment they were designed and implemented into.

Golf course design provided a strong connection between you and your father. Did it also provide an opportunity to assert your independence?

My father wasn't only my father; he was my mentor. At some point in every relationship, a mentor and his student have to separate. They both know that. For me, designing the Navatanee course in Bangkok—where the first World Cup was played—was very liberating. I went all the way to Bangkok in 1969 in order to establish my own credibility. Later, in 1975, when the Vietnam War had just ended, Jack Nicklaus declined to play in the World Cup there because it was supposedly too dangerous.

But nobody had actually thought about it. So I called General Scowcroft, the head of the National Security Council, and asked if it was really too dangerous. I didn't want to lose this opportunity. And the council told me that at that time there was no reason not to go. So they played the tournament. Johnny Miller won, the U.S. team won, and I had a good time at the pro-am. Navatanee was my first course used in professional championship play and the tournament was well publicized. That was very helpful in my career.

Your own travels and experiences seem to suggest that the game can serve as a form of adventure—not the first word that comes to mind when most folks think about golf . . .

Any game anywhere is an adventure. But going to distant locations and playing a round of golf in a totally alien context—like in Russia or Shanghai—even though the game is familiar to you, the experience and location will be different from anything you've ever experienced before.

Tell us a little more about your own golf-related adventures. What was your wildest experience?

One day in Desaru, Malaysia, I walked across a log that had fallen in a putrid swamp, and a snake slithered away. When my guide took out his machete I knew we were in trouble. I asked him, "What's up?" He said, "It's a Krait snake." I said, "What happens if he bites you?" And the guide said, "Smoke one cigarette, and say good-bye."

When we were building the course, we cut the aerial monkey trail that winds through the forest. The monkeys were not happy; they were yelling and screaming and really giving us hell. Two weeks earlier a wild elephant had pushed over our construction shack during the night. Then we found out that tigers had been coming out of the jungle to lick the salt on the beach near the sea where we were working. On the ride out, an elephant was sleeping in the road, and my driver, Chan, stopped the jeep and climbed down and started speaking very calmly and soothingly to the elephant, and it got up and quietly walked off. I asked him what he'd done, and he said he spoke to him and asked, "Lord of the jungle, may we pass?" So I asked him how he knew the elephant understands him, and he just said: "He understands me because I respect him."

That was a difficult job. Our supervisors kept quitting.

Another wilderness experience was designing the Wild Coast Golf Course, in Transkei, South Africa. The rough plunges down into ravines, and one hole plays across a natural waterfall. A real one. If you lose your ball you don't go down there, because that's where the black mamba, a poisonous snake, lives. Wild monkeys run onto the sixth green and steal your golf ball even today.

How do you express your own adventurous experiences in your golf course designs?

One way is through heroic golf holes—similar to the great eighth at Pebble Beach, where you must be a hero to cross an ocean-filled chasm to reach the green. Heroic, to me, involves a quest on which you never give up. You may have to backpaddle and regroup, and create strategies, but it's like Odysseus. You're always out there searching. And if you go out seeking you'll find something.

In terms of a course of mine that's exciting, dramatic, interesting, and heroic, the Prince Course is top among them because you have at least seven or eight heroic holes. You must avoid the creek on the first hole, cross the chasm on the second, cross a cliff on the seventh, and avoid waterfalls on twelve, thirteen, and fifteen. That's a heroic golf course, full of lines and edges of doom.

You mentioned Odysseus's quest, but what is your own quest like?

When I go out in search of a golf design, there aren't any bridges or golf carts. Unknown animals are hanging around and they may or may not be dangerous. We enter their realm to create a much more refined trip for the golfer later on. The search for the best golf course within a given site is easier if the site is flat, like in Las Vegas. But then the quest involves creativity to produce something dramatic. The best courses are those where nature has provided the canvas and my job is to discover her secrets and reveal them, as opposed to imposing a philosophy. To me, bad golf architecture is what we call "production architecture" whereby the designer sets up the holes with thoughtless repetition.

If golf courses can tell a story like that of Odysseus, do they also have other stories to tell?

Courses reveal stories in two ways. The first will bore you to death; a golfer describing a hole-by-hole account of his round will clear out a room faster than a fire.

I like to tell a story about aesthetics. Golf is a nature walk through a garden, which in every culture is an extremely important place of sanctuary and restoration and re-creation. Jesus on the cross said, "I will see you in Paradise." The literal translation is, "I will see you in the Garden."

So you think Jesus was a golfer?

He made the courses, didn't he?

But other courses tell stories, too. I think the Princeville course tells the story of great, romantic natural wonders mixed with toughness. Las Sendas, the course we just finished in Mesa, Arizona, tells a story about not giving up. We've had several courses which stopped and were revived a couple of years later due to economic or political factors. The Moscow Country Club is the most clear example of that. In golf, when it's seventy-two holes of medal play, or eighteen holes in a match, you've got to play them all, and if you get in trouble you must keep plugging along. That's an important story. It's a metaphor for life and golf.

Let's come back to the Moscow Country Club in a moment. But first maybe you could go a little farther in explaining how you express your own stories or experiences through design elements in the way a writer or artist might use elements of their respective forms to express personal feelings or experiences.

That's when golf architecture becomes golf art, which happens at a higher level; sometimes it can be almost kitschy, but hopefully it's evocative and harmonious. I've used symbolism in this way a couple of times. I built a green in the shape of the state of Texas at Las Colinas, made a brook into the Rio Grande, and shaped a bunker like Oklahoma. That was a private joke on Dan Jenkins, who lived nearby.

I also built the Zen bunker at Princeville. I'd been working in Japan and had gone down to the temples, where I saw the sand gardens with stones in them, where people meditated. To them, those stones represent islands of time as well as the islands of Japan. To me, it looked like a bunker, so I said why not put some big stones in a hole on Kauai, which is the last major landfall off the United States (except for Alaska) before you reach Japan. This was in 1970, and the Japanese had not yet come to play golf in the

States, but I knew they were going to. They saw the Zen bunker as a bridge, a welcome. They thought it was fun. In one sense, Zen is existential; meditation is a highly useful discipline for finding oneself. On the other hand, it can be a joke on you in the cosmic sense.

I try to design golf courses that will fascinate people so they'll want to play them many times and learn the depths and meanings of the courses' stories, their subtext, their poetry. There are many ways to play my golf courses. My style is very complex. You have to engage the holes, because they have character. You have all these choices, and every day there's different ones, so the story that a hole tells depends on its mood that day, and on your mood. You should struggle with the hole in your mind. It's not just an adversary to attack or defeat; you should talk to it, and listen to it.

Have we entered an age of golf architecture as golf art?

I think the 1980s marked the beginning of the new golden age in golf architecture, and the 1990s represent the environmental age. We're using less boldness, less gimmickry, and fewer natural resources today. When a natural element of the land affords the opportunity for drama—like the quarry here at Royal Westmoreland—you don't need to trick it up. It's always seemed strange to me, for example, to see bulkheads in the Wild West.

The principle of harmony in art requires that the foreground and near ground have some shape or form and color that feels harmonious when you walk into the landscape. At the level of golf art, this has to extend beyond the golf course. It's not just the frame; it's everything. For example, at the Whistler golf course, in British Columbia, Canada, in June the bunkers and the snowdrifts high in the mountains relate to each other. They're part of the same harmony, though they're miles apart. Here in Barbados, the white-faced bunkers relate visually to the puffball clouds that float by overhead.

How should golfers view a course architect? Are you our ally or our adversary?

If you read my book *Golf by Design* carefully, it will teach you some of my tendencies and those of other golf architects to set up a series of challenges, risks, and rewards in a golf layout, and you'll see how and why we do that. You alone still have to play the course and make the shots, but at least you'll have a focus. And I think people with a focus always play better. In that sense I'm your ally.

In terms of the game itself, I'm your adversary. I will set up challenges that may frustrate you if you don't pay attention. But strategically I'm not a penal architect, like Pete Dye. I don't say "death or glory" very often. I'll occasionally use a penal element if it happens to be there, but basically I try to give every player—men, women, children, old and young, high and low handicaps—options in playing a hole.

Being a golf architect is a bit like being a stagehand: We set the stage for the real drama. Golf architects used to just be known within the game. They weren't known in the general sense any more than great lighting experts in the New York stage are well known by the public.

You've described yourself as an environmentalist, and stressed environmentally responsible course design. Do you feel that there are some places on the planet where a golf course just doesn't belong?

The owner and architect should share a common vision for the best results. We've actually turned down many sites because they just wouldn't become good golf courses, because they'd be forced upon the land. This is particularly true in the mountains of Japan, where it would look like an army of Kumatsus [bulldozers] had come through. I describe such designs as "accelerating geologic time"— like by twenty-five million years. Some developers will ignore the land, and we don't participate in that. We might relocate a substantial quantity of earth, but we'll do it in a way that preserves the natural elements, such as rock outcroppings, forests, and streams.

We're efficient. We're light on the land. But we're not minimal-
ists either. So-called minimalist courses—where almost nothing has
been moved in the landscape—often leave the golfer feeling unful-
filled, like leaving a Chinese restaurant still feeling hungry. That concept of minimalism is not architectural, and very few sites are that
good that you can romantically go back to basics without bulldoz-
ers. You have to build a green that drains, or you can't putt on it. Tees
have to be oriented in the right place, fairways must support heavy
mowers to cut the grass, and bunkers have to hold sand. These are
technical issues. If we have to re-create an unadorned site, we will—
as we did at Kensington and Windsor, in Florida—but we'll try to
leave it as if we haven't been there. We'll realign the terrain so that it
feels natural.

When I see a piece of land that is extraordinarily beautiful and
also conducive to golf, I get nervous—not that I should stay away
from it, but rather that I should approach it with great care. I don't
want to ruin it. I want to study it a long time and observe its character like a man getting to know a beautiful woman—he wants to
know if she's beautiful without makeup. You want to learn the true
qualities of the site before treading lightly on the land. One of the
jobs I have when I see a beautiful piece of land is to tell the owner
the truth: that he'll have to invest a certain amount of money just to
protect the beauty, and if he doesn't want to do it, or thinks he can
do it for less, I'll say let someone else do it.

In my opinion there are some great pieces of land that didn't
turn out as well as they might have—Tralee, in Ireland, for example,
a wonderful place where *Ryan's Daughter* was filmed. It was designed
by Arnold Palmer and Ed Seay. Architecturally, I could see many
ways to have made a better golf course. I'm a constructive critic as
well as a creator. I don't know what happened there. Maybe they
didn't have enough of a budget, or enough time. But they didn't get
the most out of that land, as they managed to do at other lovely
sites, such as Spring Island, South Carolina. My father's work at

Ballybunion New was not as good as it could have been. Those are extraordinary pieces of linksland. But in the case of Ballybunion I know they had almost no money, and that's very difficult. Courses like these may be remodeled later, but they can never reach the full potential they had when the site was virgin.

As an environmentalist, is it also difficult to watch the amount of development that often springs up around a golf course built in a previously pristine place? I'm thinking in particular about the thousands of hotel rooms and condos going up around your Cabo Real course, in Los Cabos, Mexico.

This has happened many times before. In Hilton Head, for example, at first people thought those golf courses were just wandering through a woodland. They were, initially, but then the houses went up and the golf courses were strung out among them, much like a suburban street. At Cabo, we purposely put the golf holes along the edges of cliffs, which is dramatic and heroic, but it also means that they can't build anything there. I don't think there'll be as many houses as you think in Los Cabos. The economy is changing radically, and who knows what the market will ask for. The plans may change. Still, my suggestion is to go there now; what will be, will be.

Overdevelopment is always a disappointment, but we have to work in the practical world. The best thing of all is pure golf—when you can design a golf course where there are no houses. If you have enough golfers in a major urban area, the market will recognize pure golf and respond. This happened recently at Granite Bay, near Sacramento. But you can't do it everywhere. The market isn't that rich.

Let's go back and talk about the Moscow Country Club. It took twenty years to build that golf course. What was the process like for you? What did it mean?

When I first saw the Reds on the greens, I knew we'd really won the cold war. In the early days of the project, it had a symbolic meaning in the West that the Russians were open enough to consider this. But it took them a long time to decide whether a golf course was a political symbol. They first thought of golf as an English game, and they didn't like the English because they held Murmansk during the Bolshevik Revolution. Golf had meanings of colonial empire. I had to explain that golf was really an old Scottish game.

On a very crude level they also pointed out that golf is a capitalist game, but we pointed out that it's not; it's a military game. Scottish soldiers played golf in India, Egypt, and elsewhere. But British soldiers were not some of their favorite historical figures. That was even more serious. But toward the end, they didn't see it as anything more than a way to provide a luxury service, and to encourage business and tourism.

In terms of the transformation of the people involved, it was a kind of reverse Doctor Zhivago. The doctor was transformed by his experiences in the Bolshevik Revolution. In the case of the golf course, because it took so long, many of the Russians involved were transformed backward to a less ideological society. Dr. Armand Hammer was the catalyst, back in 1974.

What was your toughest challenge in getting the course built?

They never gave us an accurate map. I'm a former Boy Scout, and I was walking around in the woods with a compass, and I said, "This topographical map is really off." I kept saying this and it was five years before they really trusted me. They said I was very observant.

"Is it wrong?" I asked.

"Yes. The map is incorrect."

I asked how I was supposed to do my job and they said, "We do not give correct maps to foreigners because your military will use it to attack us."

And I said, "Well, I'll give you an incorrect golf course unless you give me a correct map." Paranoia is a national science over there. But for good reason. The bunkers on the third hole in Moscow are actual bunkers from which they fought the Germans in World War II. Also, I was told that the woods approximately thirty kilometers northwest of Moscow is approximately where Napoleon's army fought. They've been attacked so many times. They had reason to give me an inaccurate map. They finally gave me a map that was so accurate they had calibrated the circumference of every single tree in the forest.

Beyond the game of golf, what did building the course mean to you personally?

I believe that if we can play a sport together then we might not kill each other. It's the Olympic ideal: Get guys communicating by having a competition through sports. And what sport do older diplomats and generals play? Golf.

In November 1979 I asked a major player, Ambassador V. Kuznetzov, how things were in Moscow. He said, "Things in Moscow are much colder than the snow in your face." A month later they attacked Afghanistan. That was the end of sports exchanges, and the project went into deep hibernation.

Six years later the Russian client called up again and said Gorbachev's in power and he wants to talk about that golf course. Then there were little things, like his government collapsing. The most positive thing I can say is that at the opening, soldiers from the Red Army came to see the course and they had to try it. If you don't build it, they'll never see it, and never try to play.

It sounds like you have very strong feelings for the Moscow course. Do you have other favorites, courses that mean particular things to you, or express specific moods?

When I want to play serious golf I go to Pine Valley, because I grew up in New Jersey and have been playing Pine Valley since I was sixteen, and I have a lot of memories. I go with friends and we play all day long and try to eat as many meals as rounds we play. It's a very difficult course—walking golf. It's like going to church: You get rein-vested with the lore and the nature of the game.

To me St. Andrews is an interesting place, but I always feel slight-ly uneasy because there are so many oddball bounces. You have to learn to laugh at the golf course, because it's certainly laughing at you.

I like the San Francisco Golf Club. I like Winged Foot because you have to hit really precise approach shots. It brings back all kinds of memories, too. That's where Tommy Armour taught me how to play. It's very evocative.

Golf courses are like outdoor churches. They're places you have a lot of memories of great matches won and lost, friends enjoyed, weather—all kinds of things come flooding back.

You communicate your love for the game and some of your memories and experiences in your book Golf by Design. *Would you like to say a few words about the book?*

I did the book for two reasons. First, I would play golf with someone at the San Francisco Golf Club who'd been playing there all his life, and I'd say "Do you usually come up short on the fifth hole?" He'd say, "How did you know?" And I'd say, "Because you see where the bunker is set fifteen yards short, but it's a high-faced bunker, the top of which obscures the fairway, and it looks like it's right in front of the green? Your eye is tricked. There's an illusion because there's no background and no reference point. It's pure ocu-lar science. You think the green is closer and you cannot make your-self hit the club you need to hit, even though you know the yardage." After such explanations people often told me, "You should write a book!" Eventually I got hubris and thought that I should write a book.

But more importantly, the book was a gift back to the game, which has been so good to me. I wanted to help people understand what architects do, just as a museum curator could explain the works of Picasso and Rembrandt in a deeper way than just as beautiful paintings. I wanted to elicit a depth of appreciation and communicate the beauty, the whole ethos of being on a golf course. I also wanted to help people play better. I wanted them to defeat me.

In a Zen-like way, I'm a master of my art, and I want to teach you my art. And if you enjoy it as I have, then I'm blessed.

22

Playing Through

SOME GUYS CONSIDER themselves lucky if they manage to play golf every other week throughout the year—at least until they hear that last year, Jeff Simonson played as much golf as they did: in twelve hours. Simonson, a thirty-eight-year-old financial planner from Clackamas, Oregon, set a Guinness world record of 468 holes in half a day. A good question is: How? A better question: Why?

Playing with just three clubs (driver, five-iron, nine-iron), and using a souped-up cart to move him along between shots, Simonson raised more than ten thousand dollars for the Portland Rescue Mission. Assistants teed up balls for him in advance at each tee box and pulled his holed putts from the cup, but Simonson swung upward of fifteen hundred times en route to beating the previous twelve-hour record by one hole. It was his third attempt: The first time, his body gave out. The second time his cart did. Simonson circled the 6,000-yard Gresham Golf Club twenty-six times, driving 110 miles and running in excess of twenty-five miles. En route, he ate half a sandwich, three candy bars, and a granola bar; drank five bottles of sports drink and two bottles of water; and went to the bathroom once, in his seventh hour. He averaged thirty-nine holes per hour while shooting bogey golf, lost twenty-five to thirty balls and three toenails, and toured the final nine holes in twelve minutes. Simonson says of his feat, "It seems to tear up your hands a bit."

As you read this, Simonson may be training to set another record—the most holes played in twelve hours without the use of a cart. But he'll only attempt the 216 holes (equivalent to running approximately thirty-six miles) if a title sponsor will put up twenty to twenty-five thousand dollars for charity. Operators are standing by.

23

Golf Architecture's Biggest Fan

IT'S EVENING AT Archipalooza, an unofficial summit of golf course architects being held at Oregon's Bandon Dunes Resort. Down in the Bunker Bar, while a gaggle of architects guzzle beer and shoot pool and discuss turf grass, Tommy Naccarato is working up a sweat. The big man hunches forward in his chair facing sixteen photographs of bunkers from golf courses around the world. To most people, the bunkers would appear pretty similar—some sand, some sod, some shadowed edges, a glimpse of linksland in the background. But to Naccarato, they're as distinctive as Victoria's Secret models.

"Kingston Heath!" he shouts suddenly in a voice that's both rough and boyish. He wipes his brow like he's executed a difficult athletic feat. Which, in a way, he has—he's just set a new Bunker Bar record by identifying thirteen of the sixteen photos. A few architects look over, amused. Although Naccarato is not, in fact, an architect (he's a forty-two-year-old union electrician from La Habra, California), he has somehow managed to penetrate the inner sanctum of this strange brotherhood of course designers, mostly through persistence, hours of study, and genuine admiration of their craft. Trading hundreds of emails and Internet postings about architecture each week has also helped.

A fourteen handicap and a golfer since the age of nineteen, Naccarato is obsessed with course design. Consider this: When he made his first pilgrimage to Pine Valley and stepped onto the tenth tee, his caddie handed him a seven-iron. Naccarato asked how far it was to the infamous "Devil's Asshole" bunker.

"128 yards," his caddie said.

"Give me the eight," Naccarato decided. "I did not come all the way here to get on the green. I came here to take on that asshole."

By doing intensive project work as an electrician. Naccarato logs major hours in a short time, stockpiles funds, and then takes off to visit golf courses and meet architects. The architects themselves— guys like Coore, Harbottle, and Doak—don't know quite what to make of him. They seem to clearly respect Naccarato, but also convey the sort of fondness folks reserve for genuine nut jobs.

Brad Klein, well-known golf architecture writer, offers Naccarato the highest praise, declaring that his stature as a golf architecture groupie is unprecedented. "The great classical architects— MacDonald, Tillinghast, and Thomas—had three things in common," Klein says. "They were outrageous characters, they were incurable drunks, and they died penniless in pursuit of their craft. Tommy Naccarato fits in perfectly with their style and enthusiasm."

24

Metaphors Be with You:
In Search of Tim Gallwey, Anti-Guru of the Inner Game

I WAS FIFTEEN years old when I first began reading books full of Zen koans—short, nonlinear parables meant to suddenly shock earnest students into enlightenment.

A monk asks the master, "What is the Buddha?"

The master replies, "Three pounds of burlap!"

And the student experiences a revelation.

Around that same time, I also picked up a book called *Inner Skiing* by Tim Gallwey with Robert Kriegel, thinking it might lead me to see more clearly and help me along my "path." While I expected Gallwey's book to improve my skiing, I also hoped it would provide other answers I needed to get on with my potentially remarkable but not fully enlightened (yet) life. But the book was a little too dense for a frenetic teenager. I put it down, figuring I'd return to it soon.

Twenty-three years later, I finally got around to rereading Gallwey's book in preparation for a magazine assignment, after an editor friend asked if I'd be interested in writing a sort of "My Search for" piece. The object of the search would be the author Tim Gallwey, who'd written *The Inner Game of Golf* in 1979—one of the seminal sports psychology books of all time, and certainly one of the most influential ever written about golf. But since publication of this widely read text, Tim Gallwey had virtually disappeared from golf's radar screen. My charge was to find out where he'd gone to, and why.

I imagined Gallwey as a reclusive, Salingeresque figure, a shy genius who'd created something almost beyond his control: a book that had touched millions but might have ultimately caused its author to retreat back into anonymity.

So I picked up a used copy of the original edition of *The Inner Game of Golf* and read it carefully so that I'd have at least a few educated questions to ask in case I successfully ferreted out the author. I was struck by how much from the book seemed familiar, and I realized that was because so many other writers and golf instructors had since borrowed many of Gallwey's original concepts. In fact, my friend Fred Shoemaker, from the Golf in the Kingdom Workshop, had worked extensively with Gallwey and was one of his disciples. In pursuing some additional reporting, I also learned that Random House, Gallwey's publisher, was planning to release revisions of Gallwey's four sports books, as well as a new book sometime in the next year or so—all of which I thought might provide the author with a reason to talk to me.

My actual search for the mysterious Gallwey does not in itself make for much of a story: I called an old friend who is the director of publicity at Random House, and she looked up his number in her Rolodex. Then I called the number and reached the author at home.

Gallwey was cagey and self-protective and slow-talking the first few times I spoke to him long distance—just as I'd hoped. It was difficult even to get him to commit to a date for our next phone conversation. After our initial contact, he also called my magazine editor seeking further reassurance about what our intentions were—as if we might have been plotting some investigative piece in which we'd misconstrue his ideas or twist his work to our own purposes. Or perhaps he was just afraid we'd reprint the worst-ever author's jacket photo from the original *The Inner Game of Golf.*

Before he agreed to even consider meeting with me in person, Gallwey also wanted to see a list of the questions I was likely to ask. A week later I faxed him a letter explaining my ideas and suggesting that I'd prefer to simply start conversing and see where it might lead. But I also mentioned that I'd want to cover a couple of specific topics—what he'd been doing all these years and why he'd given up on golf; the currently popular notions of golf as metaphor and golf as a path to enlightenment; and other aspects of what I perceived to be the Inner Game. In my fax, I casually listed a couple of dozen questions I might ask.

When I called to follow up, Gallwey admitted in his concise manner that he had trouble with some of the questions. He read down my list one question at a time, not actually answering any, but explaining why he would or wouldn't be able or willing to answer them if I ever got the chance to conduct this interview.

He was particularly irked by a couple of questions that referred to the Zen of golf, and which compared the game to a spiritual discipline. "I want to stay away from the 'mystical,'" he told me sternly. "Golf is not mystical. People can be mystical. But I've never met a person who has attained enlightenment on the golf course, or through golf. I'm amazed at how much has been written about that. How do you talk about enlightenment if you don't know what it is? The biggest obstacle to the possibility of attaining enlightenment is thinking that you know what it is. I don't want to have any part of that, except to say: Don't have any conceptions about enlightenment. Whatever you think it is, it's not that."

Then his voice softened and he told me a story about how a couple of years after *The Inner Game of Tennis* was published, a young Italian man showed up at his door one day unannounced. The man said that he'd read *The Inner Game of Tennis,* as well as other "spiritual" books, and he proclaimed that tennis was his own path to enlightenment. He offered to sweep Gallwey's tennis courts and perform other services in exchange for Gallwey's guiding him along that path.

Gallwey asked the man if he wanted to learn tennis or enlightenment.

"Both," he said, "just as you did."

Then Gallwey explained that he hadn't learned enlightenment through tennis, but the more he denied being that kind of teacher, the more convinced his visitor became that he'd found the right master, and that the author was simply testing him.

"I don't want to mix these two things," Gallwey explained to me over the phone. "I have strong feelings about the disservice of claiming to teach enlightenment. I get accused of saying that golf is 90 percent mental, but I would actually say that it's 90 to 95 percent physical. It involves a physical ball hit by a physical club swung by a physical body on physical terrain. That's the definition of golf. But that's not all people do when they play golf. People create metaphors."

Which is only a small part of what Tim Gallwey and I talked about a few months later when I flew to Los Angeles to spend a couple of days with him.

His wife, Leslye, answered the door of their modest country estate in the horsey hills forty-five minutes north of the city. A robust silver-haired man was coming down the stairs as Leslye greeted me, and though he said, "I'll go see if I can find Tim," I recognized his voice right away. It wasn't so much calculating as contemplative, I realized. And now, in person, he seemed confidently irreverent rather than stern.

We shook hands and Tim took me for a brief tour of this recently acquired property—pointing out the vegetable garden, where the tennis court would go, the old horse stalls. The stalls prompted a story: Tim had recently come across a video created by a horse trainer in which the trainer used Inner Game principles to break wild horses in less than half an hour, as opposed to the six weeks it usually took.

I asked if that was the strangest application of his principles that he'd heard of, and Tim told me about a cataract surgeon who used Inner Game methods to teach other doctors a difficult new surgical technique.

After slowly walking around the grounds we eventually eased into a couple of chairs out on the front lawn. Leaves fell from the oak trees in a cool breeze and the sun dipped behind distant hills as we settled in to talk.

Tim offered me a brief professional history—how he'd gotten interested in education as an English and philosophy student at Harvard (where he was also captain of the tennis team), taught English at Exeter, worked at an experimental college in the Midwest, turned down a dean's position at Georgetown, and eventually returned to teaching tennis as a break from academia. Late one afternoon, as he was trying to muster the energy to help a student break a bad swing habit, Gallwey experienced a revelation. Tossing balls to the student, he noticed that the man's swing had somehow managed to correct itself, and he suddenly felt let down that he'd missed his chance to teach him something useful.

"The Inner Game was born in the next moment," Tim remembered. "I became aware of my reaction and realized that I was more committed to teaching than I was to my students actually learning. If a student learned something that I didn't teach, I was disappointed. I wondered what might happen if I became more committed to students learning. So I let go of teaching. It totally changed my point of view."

Gallwey began to examine the process of teaching, focusing more on the student than on comparing the student's technique to some mechanical model of good form and analyzing the difference—which is how most sports instruction, especially golf instruction, works today. Everyone else teaching sports at that time was looking at the outer behavior of the athlete, Gallwey recalled. He began asking what goes on inside a person who is trying to learn a sport.

A lot was going on, he realized. And a lot of it was not particularly useful—such as the self-criticism, self-assessment, and major doses of doubt that many golfers would be intimately familiar with.

From this realization, Gallwey developed his concepts of Self 1 and Self 2, which constitute an integral part of Inner Game theory, and much of what Gallwey writes about in his books. He defines Self 1 as "that which has stopped listening to oneself and has accepted the views of others." It's that critical voice that calls you an idiot after you knock two tee shots into the same pond. Tim turned to me and asked, "What would you do if another guy in your foursome spoke to you the way you speak to yourself?"

Self 2, on the other hand, is the reservoir of all your abilities and talents, the Self who's in charge when you're performing in the zone. Gallwey recognized that when an athlete faced a difficult task, judgment and control (exercised by Self 1) often interfered with the athlete's natural ability to perform (carried out by Self 2). And he understood that as a teacher he was contributing to the interference. So he began exploring how he might create a more optimal internal learning environment. Gallwey points out that he based his concepts on observations of things that athletes and salesmen and writers were already experiencing, not on some grand theoretical framework.

In teaching golf and tennis and even business, which is where he currently devotes much of his professional time, Gallwey believes students can learn far more from their own experiences than from listening to some expert teaching them technique and then comparing their performance to a model. Although Gallwey professes that golf is a mechanical not a mental game, what's at issue is how you learn mechanics, and whether you can succeed in getting out of your own way. Or, in other words, quieting Self 1 so that Self 2 can learn and perform.

Lessons, Tim says, should invite the student into an experience, whether the lessons are about the short game in golf or peak performance in sales. "You can believe something, which involves faith," he explained, "or you can know something, which arises out of your own experience. Outside instruction can only take you to the level of belief. To really know something you have to experience it yourself. In traditional instruction we're too busy trying to conform to technique and we don't even know it."

Most of Gallwey's Inner Game theory arose from experiments with students. Within a couple of months of teaching tennis lessons again, Gallwey knew he was on to something—a method, not just a technique—and that it had to do with tennis and a lot more than tennis. At about the same time that he was beginning to teach the Inner Game, Gallwey was invited to a meeting of the Esalen Sports Institute, which was planning a seminar at Berkeley. He met Michael Murphy, George Leonard, several aikido masters, and "a whole bunch of gurus who were terribly impressive, spiritual, and profound."

At Esalen, Tim taught a workshop that he called "yoga tennis," but while there he saw a guy with a turban and a beard and white Indian clothes and thought to himself, *That would really be yoga tennis,* so he changed the name of his own program to the Inner Game.

Back then, Gallwey made a conscious choice to keep things simple and not go in the direction of the gurus, to not associate what he was doing with a spiritual discipline. Which is why he bristled at some of my questions on the phone.

Many people think that Gallwey preaches a kind of sports mysticism. When he suggests that to care only about the sport itself is to miss what that sport can do for you in other areas, he leaves himself open to the charge of being a guru. When I asked him whether such pronouncements don't lead us into that dangerous terrain of golf as metaphor he uncrossed his legs and sat eagerly forward in his chair.

"People who play golf create metaphors, which involves adding meaning to what is essentially a physical game," Tim said. "Almost everyone uses metaphors while playing golf. I don't want to pass judgment on the meaning someone might attach to the game, but if you do use metaphors, it's good to do so consciously. But a lot of players unconsciously see their performance on the golf course as a measure of their self-esteem, which is not healthy at all."

The thing about games, he continued, is that "we have to pretend they're important, but know that they're really not—like kids playing war who get called home to dinner. Once you think a game can really hurt you, it's no longer a game. Part of Inner Game theory involves developing awareness of the games we're playing and recognizing that sometimes—like with the self-esteem game—they're stupid."

On the same subject, Tim also explained that using metaphors involves taking something familiar to someone and using it to teach them about something they know little about—like when a golf pro encourages a beginner to sweep the ball off the tee as if with a broom. But what Gallwey has done with golf and tennis—and this is largely where he's disappeared to over the past twenty years—is to take a sport that a student knows little or nothing about and use it to teach him about what he does every day, creating a sort of anti-metaphor. In the corporate sector, Gallwey currently employs golf and tennis instruction as a means of teaching businessmen the lessons they need to learn to succeed in their own milieus.

Tim's reference to his current work seemed like the perfect segue to ask him why, if golf was still so close to his heart, and if he still believed so passionately in teaching it through Inner Game concepts, he'd dropped out of the game and hadn't published a book in twenty years.

He was baffled by my question. He thought about it for a long time before he said, "I didn't know that I'd dropped out. I didn't know that I'd ever even dropped in. Nothing has changed for me. Golf and tennis were beside the point from the beginning. They were more useful as metaphor and medium. By the time *The Inner Game of Golf* came out I was already very deeply involved with the corporate world, helping managers learn how to coach, and creating learning environments at the corporate level. I still use golf and tennis in that effort. I never left the game as a means of expressing both learning and coaching."

And why hadn't he written anything in the past two decades? Despite the fact that millions of copies of his books have been published in several languages, Gallwey views himself as an educator, not an author. He only writes books when he has something to say. His new book about work—due out a few months after my visit— would explain where Gallwey had been those twenty years.

Where we had been strategic and adversarial on the telephone, in person Tim and I fell into this deep and wide-ranging conversation with the ease of neighbors discussing weather over the back fence. Gallwey was pensive, thoughtful, sensitive, funny. Even as he explained his concepts to me, he also listened to my ideas and inquiries and used them to refine and even question his own. If Gallwey was some sort of master teacher, he was also a student in the purest sense.

Nearly three hours had gone by when Leslye brought us a couple of glasses of Cabernet and asked if I'd like to join them for dinner at a nearby sushi place. There, we spoke for several more hours, descending into the personal realm, talking about our relationships with our fathers, for example, as we sipped sake and gobbled raw tuna and California rolls.

To illustrate a point Tim told another story about a guy he knew who started playing golf by himself in the afternoons, when his early shift at work was over. After a year of playing a few times a week, the man was shooting par. When he finally went out on the course with a couple of friends, they marveled at how good he'd become in so short a time.

The man was surprised, because he thought that *par* meant average—like in the phrase *par for the course*. After his friends convinced him that he was a superlative golfer and practically ready to go out on tour, he never broke eighty-five again. As a game, golf had been easy for him, but when it meant something else, he lost his innocence and couldn't play the same way.

Eventually, Leslye insisted that they had to go home; Tim and I had an early tee time, the restaurant was closing, and if she didn't stop him, he was liable to stay up talking all night.

At 7 A.M. I met Tim in the parking lot of a fast-food joint and climbed into his car for the drive out to the Malibu Country Club. We sipped bad coffee and talked like two people on a second date, slowly working to reestablish the connection we'd formed yesterday.

The golf course nestled in the bottom of a narrow valley with the rolling terrain of the Santa Monica Mountains rising high in the distance. A frost delay had canceled the first half hour of tee times, so the pro shop was crowded and chaotic when we arrived. We checked in and then carried a couple of buckets of balls over to the practice nets that served as a driving range and began warming up.

Tim carefully lined up eight balls on the plastic grass and hit them in a slow rhythm without interruption—backswing-hit, backswing-hit, and so on. I heard the click of the balls and watched the regular plumes of Tim's breath.

I hit a few balls and tried to think about what I should be thinking about. I consulted a long menu of advice I'd received from various alternative golf pros, and then tried to be aware of what was going on with me, as Tim might have suggested. It was very confusing. Should I focus or let go? Should I begin visualizing my round or try to eliminate interference? Would it be better to harmonize the hemispheres of my brain or perhaps toss some clubs into the practice net? Pee or drink more coffee? Keep asking these stupid questions or shut up?

When the starter finally called us to the tee I headed over to load my clubs on the cart. Tim said he'd catch up with me in a minute. He continued to hit a couple more shots with his smooth, loping swing.

When I'd loaded both bags and driven the cart to the head of the path to the first tee, Tim walked methodically toward me, but then stopped at the snack bar and ordered a coffee and a hot chocolate. He fumbled for his wallet, searched for cream and sugar, stir sticks, napkins. The starter looked on impatiently, glaring at his watch and then at Tim, but Tim failed to notice. He was happy, relaxed, slightly oblivious. He set the drinks in the cart, where they sloshed all over as we drove to hole number one.

Tim's idea for our round was for us each to serve as the other's coach, using Inner Game principles to help each other become more aware of aspects of the way we played. Put simply, this involved providing each other with a focus for each shot—something like flow or follow-through or where the shoulders were aimed. Once the coach gave us our focus, our job would be to stay as aware of this factor as we could, and then rate ourselves on a scale of one to ten—not on how well we flowed or whether our shoulders aimed the correct way, but rather on how aware we were of this swing component. According to Inner Game theory, we would ultimately learn the best swing and manage to execute it without interference only by directly experiencing every aspect of it for ourselves.

All of which sounds easy and obvious, but for me it was anything but. On the first tee Tim suggested that I just focus on hitting the ball the way I wanted to—not on where it went, but on how the swing felt. Frost was melting on the sunny patches of grass and I was stiff and cold, but I swung hard at the ball and immediately worried about where it went. When Tim asked me to rate my awareness of hitting the way I'd wanted, I admitted it was pretty low, maybe a four.

For lack of anything more original, I counseled Tim to also focus on hitting the way he wanted to. His swing was smooth and graceful. He punched a long, straight drive down the right side of the fairway. As I admired it, I remembered that the result was beside the point.

"How was your awareness?" I asked.

He smiled at me. "About a six, maybe a seven," he said thoughtfully.

As he drove the cart a little wildly out to my ball, Tim suggested that I be aware of balance on this next shot. And suddenly, without my even being aware of it, Self 1 stepped in and took control. I was surprised and even a little offended that Tim had chosen balance as my focus. I interpreted this to mean that he didn't think my balance was very good—although that's always been one of the reliable foundations of my swing.

As I stood in the hard, frosty rough addressing my ball I was far more aware of my interpretation that Tim's comment implied some judgment about my balance than I was of that actual swing component. I was clearly listening to voices not my own as I stood beside where my ball sat up weirdly on the frozen grass.

I took a slow backswing and hit my next shot off the toe of the club. It squirted across the fairway and into the rough on the opposite side. I immediately felt a sharp jab of annoyance, registered my awareness of it, and then registered my awareness that this whole awareness thing was really starting to piss me off. When Tim asked how aware I'd been I confessed to about a three, and began to feel more agitated. I was also reticent to coach Tim because I felt self-conscious, and judged myself to be clumsy and ineffective in that role. Self 1 was a tenacious adversary.

Sensing my frustration, on the next hole Tim recommended that I try an exercise from *The Inner Game of Golf* that he called "back-hit-stop," which was designed to distract Self 1 from interfering so that the natural athleticism of Self 2 could execute the shot.

But even as I tried this, the critical voice in my head was unable to let go of judgment, and I flubbed my next couple of shots. This went on for three more holes. Standing on the tee of a lovely downhill par three a couple of minutes later, my frustration inflating within me, Tim calmly offered another focus and I knew I couldn't take any more. I fired Tim Gallwey—perhaps one of the greatest instructors in sports history—as my coach.

Tim was awfully surprised; he asked if I might be willing to still receive some coaching from him if he only offered it when asked, so that I could be in control of the relationship. I agreed because I really wanted to learn something from Tim and move beyond my interferences.

Over the next couple of holes my tension sloughed away. I noticed birdsong filling the canyon and the way the sun had climbed to the center of the sky and begun steaming the moisture from the vegetation. I eventually asked Tim for his coaching advice, and freely offered up focuses for each of his shots. After execution, we compared our awareness ratings out loud. We fell into a rhythm, and I began to understand how this whole thing could work. Performance fell at the feet of awareness, and we talked and encouraged each other and the day blossomed into all I'd hoped it might be.

Throughout the round Tim played with great humor, humility, and camaraderie. On several occasions, he mistakenly replaced his clubs in my bag, or put his clubhead cover on my driver, or worried about having lost an iron that was right in front of him. I found this utterly charming. Tim played with the pure abandon of a teenager—not a teenager worried about what things meant and why they weren't different, but a teen lost in pure play, and I thought to myself: *Of course!*

Afterward, on the sunny drive back out the canyon, we processed our experience a little bit. Tim observed that to the extent I'd allowed him to coach me, he'd tried to take the place of Self 1 by assuming the responsibility for where I should focus my attention so I'd be free to let Self 2 just play. We both recognized how difficult this had been for me, and Tim suggested that I might take away from this experience a greater willingness to be a student, to know that I can give myself over to a coach—or even to my more natural and uncritical self—and still be free. That it's okay to trust, though I still needed to reach conclusions based on my own experiences.

Tim said he'd experienced being a student of golf and a student of coaching, and he admitted to having learned a lot during the day.

He dropped me off back at my own car and we said good-bye in the Burger King parking lot, surrounded by mountains that were unfamiliar to me. I watched until his car disappeared down the road then climbed into my own and went on my way.

25

Signature Hole

IF YOU WERE anything like me in high school, you spent a lot of time during history class drawing impossibly difficult golf holes in your notebook. What avid golfer doesn't imagine he could design a great layout?

This past year, Phoenix-based golf course architect Greg Nash—Billy Caspar's partner, and designer of more than fifty courses—offered me the chance to quit daydreaming and step up to the drawing board. Nash agreed to build one golf hole of entirely my creation into a layout he was designing near Las Vegas.

Nash was tired of golfers misunderstanding the difficult nature of course design. He was fed up with businessmen and surgeons proffering opinions about why the fourth hole was too narrow on one of his layouts, or complaining that he should have flattened that bunker by the twelfth green. In providing a writer with the chance to create one-eighteenth of a golf course, Greg hoped that I'd communicate to folks what his profession is really like. He hoped I'd express some of the intricacies, frustrations, and endless challenges faced by course architects. Because, as Greg says, "A lot of people don't know spit from apple butter about golf course design."

FIRST VISIT: JANUARY 29

I met Greg in person on the morning of my first site visit, when he picked me up at the Las Vegas airport. I'd expected a strapping, gray-haired statesman; instead, I was greeted by a slightly grizzled rock star wearing jeans, dusty cowboy boots, a black leather jacket, and Kenneth Cole shades.

As we drove to the future home of Del Webb's Revere at Anthem Golf Course, in nearby Henderson, Greg handed me a topo map and told me a little about the site, which he described as awesome. Although the course was being built amid a subdivision, the golf holes played through the bottoms of a series of canyons. The houses were mostly confined to the mesa tops. Greg explained that most subdivision layouts force you to invent the entire topography; here, the canyon system provided challenging natural terrain that would allow us to be more creative and spontaneous.

Greg suggested that I look at the land as it existed and think about what we'd need to do to create a great golf hole, starting from the tees. Then he told me I'd be designing the eleventh hole, a par five of approximately 620 yards.

As we drove through the front gate, the site—a large swath of desert stripped clean of vegetation—struck me as bleak. Although the canyons were dramatic, the place depressed me. Greg had already routed the golf holes and erected stakes to mark the centerlines of the fairways. As dust blew across the mesa, I wondered what was really left for me to do.

Greg maneuvered his four-by-four across the golf course and explained how the builders would dozer off the topmost layer of rocky soil and eventually deposit six inches of fluffy fill dirt before grassing the holes. They'd eventually plant sage, yuccas, and other natural desert vegetation to make the course blend in with its surroundings, and they'd even edge a few fairways with stately Mondelle pines as aesthetic accents. He referred obliquely to dynamiting rock, laying irrigation pipe, moving dirt, engineering water features, and performing a dozen other processes I'd never considered back in history class. And that was only a glimpse of the real work involved. "I'm not sure what our budget is, exactly, but it's at least ten million," he said.

When we reached the deep pit that would someday become the eleventh hole, Greg excused himself to confer with a couple of his associates about cart path locations, subcontractors, heavy machinery, and mowable slope angles. I was left to consider my artistic canvas and wait for the land to begin speaking to me.

Number eleven began on the rim of a high, flat mesa, and descended a hundred feet down a saddle into a winding canyon. In the distance, the Vegas skyline and a range of tall, notched mountains shimmered in the dusty sky. Not far from the future teeing areas, the mesa dropped over a sheer cliff that would have made for a fantastic tee box, but I saw the ropes and stakes marking it out as a housing site. I'd encountered my first design limitation, and I began to understand the kinds of compromises that Greg must face.

The very bottom of the canyon, which was crossed by a dry wash, flowed like an ancient riverbed, winding from side to side. I liked this organic movement, except for where a slope descending on the left side of the hole cut off the view to where the green was located.

My mind wrapped itself around launch angles and potential hazards. I tried to imagine what this wide expanse could look like as a golf hole. I wanted it to blend naturally into the landscape, but what kind of design elements would reflect this canyon topography while simultaneously expressing some of my own personal philosophies about golf—all without seeming hokey or tricked up?

I knew that my hole called for a rugged western sort of styling, and I thought about the Grand Canyon, which lay not far from here to the southeast. I imagined a golf hole in which the fairways consisted of multilevel tiers, like mesas juxtaposed against each other— just like what I saw on the horizon, too.

Looking out at the mountains, I also noticed a V-shaped notch, and wondered: Why not cut a corresponding V out of the middle of that left slope, thereby allowing golfers to see and play toward the green, and simultaneously creating a desert island floating in the middle of the fairway?

Later that afternoon, as we drove back toward the airport, I described my still-forming ideas to Greg. He offered a reserved consent, and told me he'd fax me a sketch later in the week. When it arrived, it captured the essence of my vision. We tweaked it and discussed it, and Greg approved this preliminary plan.

SECOND VISIT: FEBRUARY 20

As soon as we drove out to the eleventh hole, we knew it didn't look anything like what I'd described to Greg and what he'd sketched in response. Where I'd called for a steep cut that divided the fairway into flat upper and lower tiers, there was only a continuous slope. The notch in the left hillside had not been cut. Things looked much as they had on my first visit, except that the rocky cover material had been peeled off and hauled away.

Greg was calm at first. He explained how things come up—you want to cut something but you hit solid bedrock; or the shapers have a different vision of what you describe to them. "Sometimes you just have to deal with it and compromise and be creative. Which is why an architect has to be out on the job," Greg said. I sensed he was trying to tell me why this golf hole would never look anything like I'd planned.

But then he picked up his cell phone, and his mild, professorial manner disappeared. "They got this all screwed up," he shouted at someone. "How are they saying what's drawn here is out there?" He held up his sketch for emphasis.

Soon, shapers and dozer drivers and construction foremen appeared out of the desert and converged on Greg's truck.

"Didn't anybody go over this? Anyone?" he yelled. He was livid, too, that someone had hauled away the dirt they'd scraped off the fairway. Greg had intended to use that to build our tiers.

It was clear that nobody had any idea what the hole was supposed to look like, but they each explained why things weren't their fault. Greg smiled. When he showed them the drawing and described my vision, the construction foreman said, "Wow. That'll look really cool."

We drove up to the tees while the dozer operator started making the V-cut and someone arranged to have a bunch of dirt hauled

back up the slope. Greg barked into his cell phone as he drove, dealing with a raft of other mistakes and miscommunications on other
holes—all in a day's work, I understood. I also saw that he wasn't
really angry, but acting that way helped get things done.

We spend about five minutes looking at tee boxes, half a dozen
of which cascaded from the mesa top down the saddle. A few more
lay across the wash that crossed in front of the fairway and wound
around to define the left side of the hole. I offered a couple of comments and Greg took notes, but we knew it was the terrain here that
would dictate the best tee box locations.

Just before we quit for the day, Greg mentioned that I should
start thinking about the green. But I already had an idea of what I
wanted. I handed him a copy of my first golf book, *Beyond the
Fairway,* for which I'd designed the cover. It depicted a golf green
shaped into the Japanese yin/yang symbol, conveying what I consider the Zen aspect of golf. I asked whether we might re-create the
symbol, using the green as one half, and a bunker curled up against
it as the other.

Greg looked at the book and said, neutrally, "We could do that."

THIRD VISIT: MARCH 11

Shane Whitcomb, Greg's design associate, was waiting for us in
his truck when we arrived. We drove out to number eleven, past
where a machine was screening dirt twenty-four hours a day for the
120,000 square yards they'd need to plate the holes. As we
approached my hole from behind the green, the fairway still looked
wrong—mostly slope. When I mentioned this, Greg said, "That
might be the part where we have to say we did the best we could."

We drove right up to the future putting surface and consulted
the diagram I'd sent Greg, and he asked how I thought it looked.
When I said that some of the bunker lines needed sharpening, Shane
handed me a can of spray paint. I revised the shape and painted the
turf island into the middle. With the bunker stepped below the
green, the execution represented an abstract interpretation of my
concept, and it looked very cool.

Then we drove up to the tees, which had been mostly roughed in as we'd decided, except for the leftmost tee, which wasn't there. I'd sited this tee to make the carry seem farther because of the angle to the fairway. We set stakes for this tee, and then looked out at the hole: from here, number eleven had begun to look like a golf hole—a beautiful and daunting par five.

From this perspective, the fairway tiers also looked more pronounced, and I noticed a third tier way down to the left, just before the fairway fell off into the wash. Greg explained that this tier had appeared when they ran out of dirt. To me, it greatly enhanced the effect I was looking for, a happy accident.

Greg and Shane drove down the future cart path, but I walked to the first landing area, where the fairway tiers converged into a swale. From this spot, you could hit to the left of the fairway island, through the V-cut, directly toward the amphitheater green, although you couldn't reach it yet. Once you passed through the cut, the hole was turfed all the way to the pin. You could also play a more conservative shot to the right of the island, to another tier that would offer a challenging third shot over a faced ridge lined with yuccas, and the yang of the bunker. If you mis-hit your second shot and landed too close to the island, you'd have to knock out to one of the fairways to have an approach to the green.

Three ridges on the hole—up on the mesa top; on the right side of the island; and fronting the right side of the green—unified the movement of the hole. Three arrangements of yuccas (separating the fairway tiers; atop the island; and fronting the green) added to the sense of flow. With luck, a small tier on the green would reiterate the tier theme established on the fairway.

I offered a few recommendations for tweaking number eleven, and then Shane asked if I wanted to play my hole. While Greg feigned anger and amazement to his workers over various glitches throughout the golf course, Shane and I drove up to the tees to hit a few balls with beater clubs. I teed up on a pinch of desert sand and crushed my first drive down the center before hitting two more balls that caromed off to the right. Shane hooked a couple into the wash on the left, and we took off after them.

Even from where my tee shot landed, it was a long way to the hole. I aimed my second shot into the V-cut and airmailed it onto the desert island. Shane offered me a favorable ruling, and after dropping in the dirt beside the island, I knocked a five-iron onto the green. Shane suggested we leave the ball buried there for posterity.

I had—more or less—managed to par The Revere at Anthem's 620-yard eleventh hole by hitting driver, driver, five-iron. I realized, happily, how tough this hole really played.

FINAL VISIT: JUNE 24

Greg called in the middle of June to suggest that I visit Anthem one last time before they started plating the holes with clean dirt. Driving in, the site looked completely different, with new roads laid out, housing foundations rising, and a forest of boxed trees awaiting planting. Two holes had already been grassed, and I could only imagine how much more work had occurred to bring them to that point.

The first thing I noticed on number eleven was that the trees I'd called for had been planted, but not quite how I'd meant. I was happy to see that the mesa effect worked well now, except from the frontmost tees, where the drop-off was mostly slope. You could see and feel the hole's shot values, and appreciate the drama of the island from the first landing area.

We spent much of that day working on the green with Wayne Ward, Greg's expert shaper. Wayne wore a cap that said BETTY FORD CLINIC OUTPATIENT, and handled a tractor like he'd been born on it. Wayne's challenge was to level out the green so as to minimize unwanted sloping. While he pushed dirt around and surveyed the results, Greg and I drove up to the tees for a final look. From the daunting back tees, the slow river motion of the hole flowed beautifully and the fairway tiers and the desert island built anticipation for the approach to a green that would also startle and delight. Even without grass, Greg had already transformed this site into a crafted work of art.

On our way back to the green, I mentioned that some of the trees seemed a bit off, and that I thought we could make the lines crisper with a couple more. Greg got on the phone and called for more pines, and they arrived in a tractor bucket, and we placed them in such a way that they moved your eye along the correct route for playing the hole. When we stepped back and looked, the entire aspect of the hole was improved.

Wayne was gone when we returned to the green.

"He's either confident or afraid," Greg said. Then he added that he would put Wayne up against any tractor driver in the country.

When we surveyed it, the green still dropped a bit strongly from the left edge, which would cause golf balls to roll toward the middle of the six-thousand-square-foot surface. But knowing how far golfers would have traveled to reach this green—over some very rough terrain—that seemed the least we could do for them.

FINAL IMPRESSIONS

At the time of this writing, the design and construction of Del Webb's excellent Revere at Anthem Golf Course is complete. Now it's all up to the grass, which has a few more months to grow itself before the official opening.

As for my sense of whether I could really design great golf courses, I would say both maybe and no. I like to think that my eye is good and that I understand both landscape and golf well enough to blend them in smooth confluence. But I also understand that vision is the twinkly but minute part of course design. Far more time and energy goes into managing a team of supervisors and a crowd of workers, dealing with technology, solving intricate problems, compromising creatively, and occasionally yelling in just the right way to get things done. While Greg Nash is an inspired course designer, he's also an artist of another sort, and I recognize that I have little talent for that particular kind of wizardry.

Now, it's up to the critics to judge how good a designer I am. But let me just mention that any surgeons or golf writers who have complaints about number eleven can keep their opinions to themselves. Or go have some apple butter.

26

The Caddie Wore
a Rolex

THREE YEARS AGO, my friend (and self-made millionaire) Nate
Dickinson offered to pay me six thousand a month to follow a story
he believed would make a gripping book and movie. My job was to
track the story's progress, scribble notes, and wait to see whether certain events panned out in a way that would make them worth writing about. At the time, I was between book contracts and struggling
to finish a novel, and found his proposition too sweet to pass up.

Nate's story was about Jerry Minor, a forty-one-year-old golfer
who'd qualified for the U.S. Open twenty years earlier but, under the
squeeze of family pressures, had given up his tour aspirations to teach
lessons at a local muni course. Now, two decades later, Minor had
roped a sponsor and was training balls-out for Qualifying School and
his second—and likely final—shot at playing on tour. As an after-
thought, Nate admitted that he was the sponsor. And confessed that
he'd be carrying Jerry's bag. He'd even developed a title for the project: "The Caddie Wore a Rolex."

It was a good tale: In addition to the *Tin Cup* drama of Jerry's
quest, each of these men possessed something the other needed.
Jerry, blessed with astonishing natural talent, had struggled financially

most of his life. He also lacked confidence. He could spank 350-yard drives and conjure magical recovery shots from off in the tullies, but he could also blow up on the easiest holes and sabotage his own chances of winning. Jerry engendered a childlike uncertainty and seemed somehow incomplete. In many ways, he yearned to be more like Nate.

Nate was a gregarious Midas—funny, loping, the kind of guy that waiters love, a former European-tour basketball player who still got juiced on sports. He enjoyed hanging with other athletes, and after retiring at age forty-two and taking a year's sabbatical, he craved a physical job where he could work outdoors. Nate also recognized that his own greatest skill was promoting other people's talent. He'd decided that becoming a PGA Tour caddie would be fun, and he believed Jerry's ability was a fast cab to his destination.

I joined them as they scouted and played golf at various possible Q School locations to determine which best suited Jerry's game, and as they competed in several local and Nike Tour events. From the first tee, I sloughed all pretense of journalistic neutrality and cheer-led for Jerry's unlikely success. Then, when I got to know him better—witnessed his angry temper, watched him behave badly in public, and saw him abuse his caddie (who good-naturedly left Jerry to carry his own bag after such outbursts)—I began half hoping he'd fail.

But under the tutelage of sports psychologist Chuck Hogan, Jerry—not much of a philosopher—pivoted inward and began to examine his life. He quit drinking. He took on some lifelong demons in straight-up match play. Nate and Chuck weren't just remaking Jerry into a better golfer. They were shaping him into a better man. How could I not root for a guy who was retooling his entire personality under the metaphorical guise of trying to play the best golf of his life? I became vulnerably entangled with my subject; emotion replaced analysis as my tuning fork. I stood behind Jerry without realizing that he wasn't the only one being transformed.

Of course, our story was about the caddie, too. One of the most poignant moments in the project occurred at a Nike Tour event in Olympia, Washington. It was storming hard when I arrived at the golf course. Nate greeted me and we walked up to the clubhouse together to find out when play might resume. At the front door, he said he'd wait for me there, out in the rain; as a caddie, the millionaire wasn't allowed inside. This amused Nate, who always knew who he was.

For three months I walked fairways and shared meals and traveled alongside the golfer and the millionaire. Jerry played erratically, outdriving young studs half his age and then throwing petit mal tantrums when he yipped a short putt or chunked an approach into the sand. In the first round of Q School in Llano, California—a place Nate joked was where they send people in the witness protection program—Notah Begay trounced the field and Jerry Minor missed the cut by one stroke, in a play-off, thus ending what had finally become our mutual quest. It was not a failure of ability as much as of ambition. Golf only allows us to accomplish what we believe ourselves capable and deserving of.

Ultimately, I'd begun hoping that Jerry might actually sail through Q School and earn his PGA Tour card. But just by allowing myself to feel for him despite his imperfections, I had moved on to my own next round. I'd swapped out judgment for sympathy—something the best writers always seem to manage, and a lesson I'd long needed to learn.

When it was over, Jerry wasn't able to reclaim his teaching job, so he launched a new career selling windows—an apt metaphor—at which he excels. Nate succeeded in a way nobody could have foretold but which we should have figured on anyway. Through contacts he made during our sojourn, he was offered a chance to carry David Ogrin's bag on the PGA Tour, which he tried out and decided wasn't for him, after all. I used the money Nate had paid me to help with the down payment on my first house—something that had always seemed beyond my reach.

It's taken me several years to see that our strange triumvirate's time together was mostly about the vagaries of success. Quantifying victory in dollars or by golf scores, I learned, means overlooking a parallel universe in which the very best thing a man can accomplish is to be fully himself, improving upon that where possible and accepting his own—and other people's—limitations with humor and grace, as Nate always did. I also learned that at times we all need someone to help us choose the right stick.

Nate, I finally came to understand, is a man who carries things—and not just golf clubs and tees, towels and energy bars. In Jerry and me, he saw some things that needed carrying, and for a while, he toted us, too.